CULTIVATING
INNER FORCE
AND
READING PEOPLE
LIKE A BOOK

CULTIVATING INNER FORCE AND READING PEOPLE LIKE A BOOK

by
Kosol Ouch
and
Jerry Evans II

E-BookTime LLC
Montgomery Alabama

Cultivating Inner Force
And
Reading People Like A Book

Library of Congress Control Number: 2005923652

ISBN: 1-59824-007-2

Published March 2005
E-BookTime, LLC
6598 Pumpkin Road
Montgomery, AL 36108
www.e-booktime.com

Dedication

I hope you enjoy this book. It is dedicated to all those who want to live multidimensionally. I dedicate this book to my wife Koeun Noun Ouch and also to all my light worker friends. Thanks to Carlos Sanchez, Jake Tepac, Jerry Evans II, Tim and Ben for all their hard work which helped make this book possible.

Thank You,

Kosol Ouch

Contents

I   Aura Introduction 9
II   Cultivating Inner Force................................. 10
III   Aura Recharging Method 12
IV   Methods For Seeing The Aura 24
V   Reading The Aura.. 26
VI   Actual Aura Readings 28
VII   Aura Camera 115
VIII   Healing 116
IX   Personal Testimonies.................................... 121
X   Telepathic Talk 144
XI   Stargate Travel 146
XII   Stargate Experience...................................... 154

        Kosol Wedding Pictures 177

I   Aura Introduction

What is the human aura? Your aura is the energy field around your person and always reflects your state of being. Think of it as just an electrical emanation around you, like a cloud of energy. Every thought and emotion you have is somehow reflected across this field of energy we call the auric field. The auric field consists of several layers, and each layer has a corresponding range of information and reality that it reflects. For example the second layer of the auric field is where emotional energy can be observed. So be aware of your thoughts and emotions reflecting your spiritual and physical bodies. The more positive you are the more positive your energy is emanating itself. One who can see your aura can not necessarily read your thoughts, but can certainly know what mood you are in by what your aura range and its colors are. For example, white gives off light and is closest to the body because it is the color that comes from our Spirit. Emotion has more bands of color added on. Everyone's aura is just as unique as they are themselves.

Being able to see and read the aura is a great way to help others understand themselves better, and is as great tool for personal growth as well. It can also be very practical when conducting energy healings on people. There are various methods that can be used to see the aura, but just like building a house you want to start with a strong foundation. This can be done by cultivating your inner force.

II   Cultivating Inner Force

Everyone has the ability to see the aura, it just depends on their level of sensitivity to it. Some can see it naturally while others must practice. Either way, a very practical way to build upon (or begin building) these skills is to cultivate what I call your "inner force". This simply means strengthening the power and range of your own energy and aura, which then produces natural side effects such as being able to sense and see auras. It is exactly like weightlifting. The more weights you lift, and the more often you practice, the natural side effects are that you become stronger and bigger and are able to do more things physically. Cultivating your inner force is the exact same thing but on a spiritual and energetic level.

The first effect or "level one" of cultivating your inner power is the ability to heal others. You become a natural channel for healing energy which can be used on yourself and others. The second level is sensitivity to the aura. This means that you will become more naturally sensitive to the aura and energies of others. This can come in the form of feelings, insights, sensations (such as heat or cold), etc. You just have a greater awareness and sensitivity to the auras of others. The third level is where you can actually see the aura. The fourth level is where you begin to see and communicate with your spiritual guides and other entities existing in higher dimensions of energy (remember, your aura itself is simply energy vibrating at a certain rate just like everything else). From this point you can continue to cultivate your inner force and continue to reap the natural rewards as a result. There is no limit, and the more you practice the more enlightened, empowered, and skilled you become.

Some people have these skills already at various levels. For example some people can speak to their guides but cannot heal. Or others may see the aura but not their guides. You can even just skip to the chapter on seeing auras if you want, but by cultivating your inner force you being building a strong foundation and then each of these abilities will follow sequentially and naturally. That is why I included it in this book. It is up to you of course how much you want to practice, and how serious you are.

So now of course you must be asking, how exactly do I build and cultivate this inner force? This can be done through a very simple but effective meditative technique explained in the next chapter.

III   Aura Recharging Method

The basics of this method are quite simple. You are simply collecting energy and then channeling it into a certain point of your body. This point is where your 3rd chakras connect, around your solar plex. This particular point in your body is like an energetic power plant. By building up energy in this area you increase the power of your entire aura, and the more you practice the stronger your energy is. You not only feel great, energized, and happy, you also begin to naturally cultivate the ability to see auras. There is actually much more information regarding this technique which is in my other book entitled "Stargate Ascension Project". But for the purposes of this book I am limiting the information for the context of being able to see and read auras.

Here are the mechanics of the meditation:

Preparation

1.   Find a comfortable position to sit in. You may sit in a chair or on the ground kneeling, in a half lotus sitting position, or even laying down. The important thing is that you are comfortable, and try to keep your back straight.

2.   Relax and close your eyes

3.   Now, visualize a sun about the size of a basketball. Place this sun about 4-6 feet above you. Make sure you have a good

idea of where the sun is and what it looks like. It can be any color or colors. Imagine it is radiating with light and energy.

4.   Next, visualize another sun again the size of a basketball. Place this sun 4-6 feet below you. Again, just be aware of where it is and what color(s) you choose to make it. Imagine it is radiating with light and energy.

5.   Now, visualize a 3rd sun. This sun is about the size of your fist and will be located in your higher chest area, between the 4th and 5th chakras. This area is often referred to as the soul seat. The color of this sun can also be any color(s).

6.   Finally, visualize a 4th sun, right in the center your body where the solar region is. This is right where your 3rd chakras connect. Make this sun the size of your fist as well.

7.   Touch your tongue to the roof of your mouth. This creates a circuit of energy and can help ground your energy during this exercise. It can be any part of your tongue making contact with any part of the roof of your mouth, as long as it is comfortable and not distracting.

For the simplicity of explaining the following procedures, I will refer to each of the suns as follows:

1st Sun = Sun below you
2nd Sun = Soul Seat sun
3rd Sun = Solar Plex Sun
4th Sun = Sun Above you

Lower Sun

8.   Inhale slowly and deeply through your nose, and imagine that a beam of liquid light is beaming from the 1st sun (below you), straight into the 2nd sun (soul seat). Imagine the 2nd sun rotating in the direction of your choice.

9.　　Hold your breath for 3-5 seconds and while you are holding your breath, imagine that the 2nd sun is collecting energy while continuing to rotate and radiate energy in all directions.

10.　　Now, bring both of your hands in front of your solar plex (palms facing the body)

11.　　Exhale through your nose, and as you do imagine the liquid light energy pouring from the 2nd sun down your arms, out of your hands, and into the 3rd sun. Imagine the 3rd sun rotating, collecting the energy, and radiating with light and energy.

12.　　Do this 20 times

Higher Sun

13.　　Inhale through your nose, and imagine that a beam of liquid light is beaming down from the 4th sun (above you), straight into the 2nd sun (soul seat). Imagine the 2nd sun rotating in the direction of your choice.

14.　　Hold your breath for 3-5 seconds and while you are holding your breath, imagine that the 2nd sun (soul seat) is collecting energy while continuing to rotate and radiate energy in all directions.

15.　　Again, bring both of your hands to the solar plex area (palms facing the body).

16.　　Exhale through your nose, and as you do imagine the liquid light energy pouring from the 2nd sun down your arms, out of your hands, and into the 3rd sun. Imagine the 3rd sun rotating, collecting the energy, and radiating with light and energy.

17.　　Do this 20 times

Final

The final part involves washing, cleansing, and re-charging your energy (aura) so that you are refreshed and re-vitalized. For this, you can now ignore the solar plex sun. Instead, visualize a new one right in the center of your brain where the hypothalamus gland is located.

18.   Inhale, and imagine a beam of liquid energy from the 1st sun (lower sun) shooting straight up into the new sun in your head.

19.   Hold your breath for 3-5 seconds, and as you do imagine this sun gathering energy, rotating, and radiating both light and energy.

20.   Exhale, and as you do imagine energy (any color) shooting out of the top of your head about 3-5 feet into the air, and then falling down all around you just like a water fountain. Imagine it cleansing your aura, your body, your organs, etc. Imagine yourself being immersed in this cleansing energy as it flows down over, around, and through you.

21.   Do this 5-10 times.

** Note that during this final cleansing method (the energy waterfall) you do not draw in energy from the sun above you, only from the sun below you.

This is all there is to it. Here is a symbolic descriptive summary of what you are doing. You are collecting energy from the heavens and earth into your chest area, and then shooting it into your solar plex region. Then, you cleanse your entire Aura by collecting energy from the earth into the center of your head, and then shooting it out like a waterfall of energy. This waterfall of energy washes and re-vitalizes your aura after collecting all that energy.

Illustrated Summary

(tongue to roof of mouth)

Meditator, remember to keep your tongue touching the roof of your mouth to complete the energy circuit in your body and also to make sure you're not using your mouth to speak or breath.

This is the Recharging Method. It is a simple meditative form that, when used, will work to balance your chi (Human Energy Field or aura) which gives energy, promotes healing and opens your chakras so they can absorb more of the Universal Energy Field, Recharging should always be done by a Facilitator after a Stargate session. Stargating can be very draining on the Facilitator and it's vitally important that they recharge after each session to keep their energy level up.

Start out by sitting indian-style or lotus-style on a pillow on the floor. Visualize the three suns; one above you (representing the sun in the sky) one below you (the Earth's core) and one at your Soul Seat (half-way between your throat and the center of your chest) all spinning in the same direction.

The direction doesn't matter as long as they are all the same.

Begin by inhaling as deep as you can, visualizing light energy from the Earth below shooting up your spine and into your Soul Seat sun. I like to motion my hands up to my chest as if I'm pulling the energy up and into my Soul Seat. Hold the breath for a few seconds (whatever is comfortable for you) and chant your Soul Mantra (OHM RAMA if you don't know). Imagine your sun spinning.

Raise your hands to either side of your head. Exhale the breath while repeating your Mantra and push the energy up your arms, through your fingertips and into your head. Imagine a small sun in the center of your head absorbing this energy. This is your third eye. Repeat this however many times as you like.

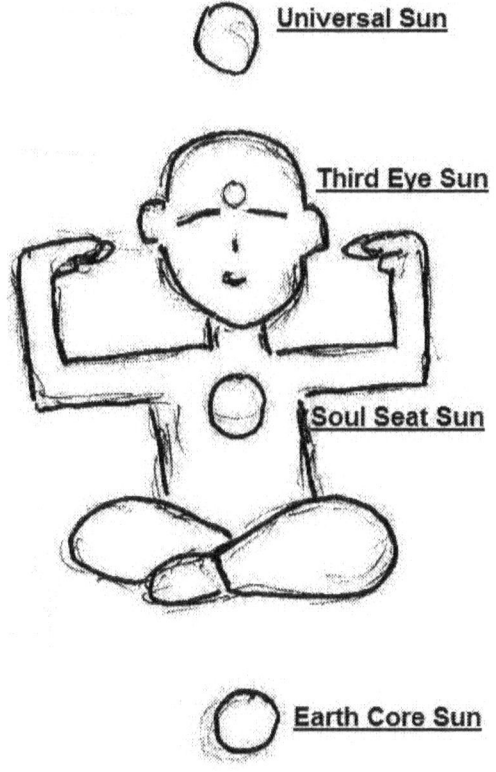

Note: You will eventually begin to feel your aura coming out of your fingertips. You will feel it against your skin. Move your hands around a little and see if you can feel the touch of your aura!

Next your going to absorb energy from the Universal Energy Field by visualizing light energy shooting from the sun above you through your head and down into your Soul Seat sun. I like to reach my hands above my head and pull down the energy into my chest at the right area. Hold the breath, chant Mantra, raise arms and release the breath with the energy moving through your arms and into your head as before.

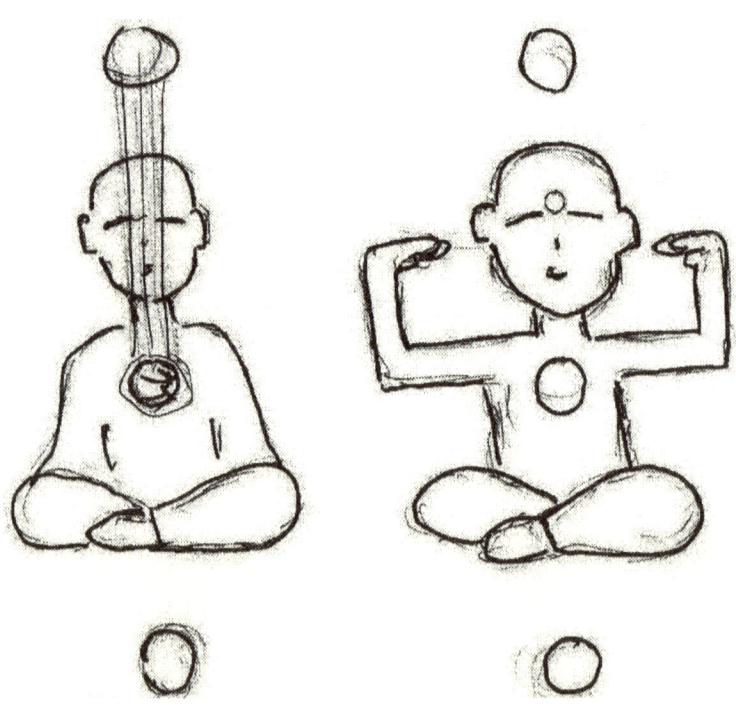

The third step is holding breathes. Just breath in, visualize your sun spinning, chant your mantra and breath out. About the same number of times as the first two steps.

The last step is called the Fountain breath. You must be careful about this step. Do not do this more than 5 cycles when you are beginning. After a lot of experience you can slowly raise this amount to 10 or more but be careful and never go above 21 cycles. When doing this step, if you ever hear a "pop" In your head, it is time to stop. This is your pineal, hypothymus and pituitary glands growing and activating. A little pop is okay but if you keep doing this you can crack your skull and die. So use much caution.

The Fountain breath cycle is inhaling as you draw energy from the Earth Core sun up your spine and into your head. Visualize a small sun in the center of your head about the size of a golf ball. Imagine a line from ear to ear and the middle of your forehead to the back and where they intersect, this is the correct place. Hold the breath, chant your mantra and release pushing the energy up and out the top of your head 4-6 feet high and then running down all over like a fountain. Repeat a few times.

Note: How many cycles you do is not very important. You can just go until you feel right. I like to do about 5-5-5-5 for a quick recharge (that's five below, five above, 5 holding and 5 fountain breaths) or more like 30-30-30-10 for a longer, more intense session. You can do it as long as you like except the Fountain breaths.

Only do 5 – 10 Fountain breaths for first year!

You may also add some cooling breaths at the end for a longer meditative session.

After using the Recharging Method you should feel energized and possibly a little buzzed. This is a natural high from absorbing energy into your being. Now is a good time to practice seeing your aura as it will be much stronger than normal immediately after recharging. Use this method each day and with practicing to see your aura you should be seeing auras and experiencing real healing in only a few months time if not faster!

IV   Methods For Seeing The Aura

Methods for seeing the aura are really quite simple, they just take practice and persistence. Another important thing is experimentation, try new things and see what helps you and works for you.

One method is to situate yourself in a room with soft or natural lighting, nothing extremely bright like fluorescent lamps. Have someone stand against the wall about 4-5 feet away from you. Focus your concentration on the wall behind the person. Pick a spot to focus on and hold your concentration there. Eventually (usually just a few seconds) you will see a slight haze of energy around the person's body. It may be white, or it may have color, it just depends on your own natural abilities. Also try focusing on the actual outline of the person, staring at a point just above their head, or shoulders, etc. Try to see the actual outline and see what happens. Just practice and experiment with different ways. Don't strain your eyes, just focus on a spot and you'll naturally begin to see the aura. Seeing it is a natural ability, you're just re-training yourself to use it. (You can use this technique on yourself too, sitting in front of a mirror).

Another method is to use a contrast of background colors. Place a black cloth or blanket on the ground and then stare at your hands (palms facing you). Look at the space between your fingers, or pick a point beyond your hands and use your peripheral vision. Just practice until you start to see a dark haze around your hands. Then, move your hands to a lighter background (such as white). You can use the wall, or another cloth. With practice, you'll start to see color when using the light background. In this method you're just training to see the aura using different background colors. By using a contrast in colors you are training your eyes to be more sensitive.

Another method is to place your hands in front of you, palms facing inwards. Have your fingers pointing at each other but not touching. Use a light background such as white, or against the sky. Now, move your hands up and down in opposite directions. Soon you will see a haze of energy around your hands, and also strands of energy jumping between your finger tips. This is another great way to practice seeing the aura.

Practice and persistence is the key. Each day when you're walking, or resting, or watching TV, just trying seeing the aura around everything. Everything is made of energy has an aura. The point of this book is to give you the abilities to see and read the human aura. You don't necessarily have to see the aura in order to read it, but it is helpful. This is because the aura contains colors and you can use these as indicators. There are many interpretations of each color, which I won't describe in this book. There are many books out there on interpreting the colors which you should definitely research. Again, I am trying to cultivate the inherent ability within each one of use that we all have.

V   Reading The Aura

Until you can see the aura and its colors, you can practice reading it through intuition and feeling, imagination, common sense, your five senses, and free will.

Now the first order of things, you MUST let go of judgment, right or wrong thinking and attitude, failure and success...reward and punishment. You must use my scale of grading, a system of 1-13, where 13 is a perfect reading. This will encourage a positive practice state of mind. Remember practice is the key, and be playful with it. Say what you see...from your first imagination and stick with that imagery and then more imagery would follow. Say what you see, hear, smell, feel, taste and what you are experiencing...plus free will, creativity, and common sense.

Be brave in your reading, (don't think you are going to be wrong because it doesn't make sense, remember you are just a reporter of the situation or mirror, that's all). Say the things you see, even if it doesn't make sense to you. The person will understand what you mean, you will be a mirror and you are giving them a reflection. You must destroy all limited belief systems, such as... you can not do it type of attitude, remember treat it like a child's game. Don't say you are right or wrong in your reading. Use the score board of my grading system. It is like an Olympic game...remember...don't ever judge. Just be an objective reporter.

When you read, it is an entertainment session, that is the attitude that you should have. Never be serious, otherwise you will lose the psychic connection with the person you are attuning to. Remember 'super power' development is a science of child play. Your imagination is the key to becoming multidimensional in existence with its infinite possibilities.

Now I want all of you to try it on one another, and the person who is being read is the guide and teacher of the person who is doing the reading. Then switch roles, and don't forget to grade each other. Then later switch partners...remember it is all a game of imagination, children having fun, but it will become real and accurate as you play the game more and more. Then you will be able to read each other like a book, then you can read me to.

Again, the key is: no right or wrong attitude, it is only a game attitude, common sense, free will creative imagination along with being open to infinite possibilities. Five senses...see, hear, smell, taste, feel, and touch. No limits and use the 1-10, 13 being perfect grading system. Also humor (laughter as well) and say what you see and experience from your imagination, through your five senses. Let it be wild...everything goes.

VI   Actual Aura Readings

On my website,

http://www.homestead.com/_allaboutlife/Index.html

I receive requests for aura readings which I accommodate. With each person's permission I posted their reading on the website. These are actual readings from the website and I just want to give you an idea of a real life aura reading and what it is like. You don't need to be in front of someone to read their aura. Once you cultivate the skill, you can do it from anywhere in the world over the phone, the internet, etc. This just depends on how much you practice and skilled you become. Read these and use them for inspiration and example, these are real readings I did for real people. Here are direct examples from my website. Note that the content was edited for grammar, but not altered.

Example #1

Hello Sharon, nice to meet you. Well, I've got much to tell you about your aura, so let's begin, shall we? Well for what I see in your auric fields, the orange color is dominant, with green cords shaped like a nuclear sign around you. Further more there seems to be a white auric field. Ok Sharon I know you've been wanting me to read your aura for a long time. Let's make it interesting and all out shall we? Ok let's get with it. Now for the orange there seems to be a sad energy associated with this orange of yours, well to tell truth the orange that is in your auric fields mean emotions. It's related to the emotional body, or the second chakras, this area is dormant in your life due to many lack of relationship fulfillments that you experienced in many lifetimes before. So in this lifetime your field will be orange and is related to the water element so empathy will move you and get your attention, so you long for emotional and sensual relationships on a full level of existence. Now, the green cords that are shaped like a nuclear sign or symbol well, green is the heart chakra's color. Well there is many variation of green but in your case the green is led toward a red green this is associated with, physical, since it is shaped like a nuclear sign or symbol, well, when this happens it means you have been in a situation that you have experienced betrayal and being used in many fashions, so you learned to root your relationship cords into your self a lot and expect from your surroundings and people that you meet in your journeys, that they will betray you in some point in your journey. So you prepared your mind and a belief structure that this is what will happen. Ok, well the good part that comes from this is that you have a dream or shall I say a goal. That goal is to be strong and be fulfilled no matter what the outcome is in your life and situation. You have learned to take enjoyment and pleasure just being alive and well in health, so you have become simple in your thought and attitude. Yes you are afraid of being led wrong when you trust someone completely, because you have experienced many times already being led wrong, and also you feel that it is expected in all of your journeys. Even new people you meet you feel that way as always it turned out to be right on many occasions, and yes there is a few turn out of wrong also, and you have lost friends that way because it hurt their feeling in a sense toward you. So you learned to adapt and feel well with it. Furthermore, you feel that you just want someone and somewhere to belong to because being strong is not easy when you feel alone. You know you have to act (put on a character) a lot, and sometimes it's not even the real you that you have to be, you have to put on a holodeck personified version of yourself. In many ways you feel guilty because you can't show your full self and expression to your friends. You are scared that they will abandon you in some fashion. You just want to be loved as you are, but under your current life situation it is sometimes hard so

29

you feel that you have to continue in such a journey until one day you have come of age in spirit or feel compatible with your self to be fully you without fear of not being accepted as you are in full spectrum of your being. And as for the white well that is related to spirit and renewal of life situations, so therefore you are being protected from bad influences by your guides. So you are under caring hands in many fashions but still you feel a need to be with someone who can read you, and know your thoughts without words and can empathetically merge with your feeling of experience of the loneliness you feel inside, and can give you a hug that will uplift you from your loneliness feeling that you have to put up with a lot of the time. You just need a guardian angel in physical form to love you, throughout all of your levels of existence, and that is all you want in life. A fulfillment of friendship, of complete love and harmonies with all of your vibrational fields.

Example # 2

Well Jude, I have much to tell you about your auric fields. First of all I want to tell you that there is much scenery in your fields like you have many recorded memories and connection feelings to many places and somehow have a sacred feeling to each one of them. All of these places give you refreshed energy of courage and earth attuning feelings to your surroundings... ok, your auric field is very red and plus yellow, orange, along with blue and pink. The most important part is there is a light being that looks like a fairy to me but big, about 14 feet tall, similar to the guardians height of 15 -16 feet. Well ok, enough of my bull let's get started, here we go... the red color, well this related to busyness, you are in a adventure quest of energy connectiveness that is related to earth and medicine of the minds for health and answer reasoning, so your physical life can have more form and more sacred admiration in it and in your surroundings, so you pretty much are attuned to nature and health. You love how you feel in the morning and how you are before you go to sleep, you are very attuned to the earth energies and its geometrical creativity. So, different scenery will energize your mind and body feelings. Mountains and water falls are the sound and the mysteries of the cosmos, like rain and ocean scenery with pyramid shaped objects etc...well, the yellow orange is related to feelings of connectedness to a thought, so you are pretty much a vivid imaginary person that means you can bring ideas in to reality from visual in the art of drawing and sculpture. So you have artistic talents and can project them into physical forms from your minds and thoughts. That is good, you are a visionary. As for the orange this also relates to your struggle of everyday life, there is a fight many time among your surroundings because the energy of a certain place drains you, so you have to fight with yourself to stay or not to stay, to help or not to helps, because you feel the need to be at a certain place and assist those who need you. But at the same time you know your energy patterns and also know your limitation of your abilities and skill and you respect that so it is hard in that perspective for you. Well as for the blue and pinks this is relates to channeling. You have developed the gift to communion with many other vibrations of light spectrums of reality. The blue is the ability to speak the truth of what you experience and the pink is the ability to listen to the heart of the matter, to say what you experience. Well as for the fairy light beings, they are your nature guides, you are connected to the elemental fairy kingdom, flowers of many colors and fruits are your likings. You do have sacred feelings for everything that you touch and see, I admire that, so the light being fairies are always leading you to sacred geometrical surrounding of some sort, they also walk with you in your dreams. Lots of times and they also show you herbs and medical herbs for healing and also methods of advanced meditations to help others and yourself so you are not alone in your adventurous journeys.

Example #3

Dear Jesse, this blue is the color that represents who you are and your life mission, that you see everything clear in your life. Also there is loneliness and sadness that accompany you on your spiritual journey. It is like this is where you have to make a decision to go on or not, apparently you are in a transitional situation with in your life. There is one close female friend that you have a very enduring bond with, somehow this relationship is based on love but lately there is a separation that cannot be prevented. It is like her physical form is far apart from you and needs time for herself, that you have lost her, she is the definition of your peace of mind. At the moment there is the sense of loneliness with this energy girl friend of yours. You also have a sensual male partner whom you share very personal time and quality time with. You and he have an intimate sharing of time on the social and feeling level. You have also a hero, a male hero in your life whom you admire and adore very much but cannot reach out to, so you can only keep secret what you feel for this person. These three energies are very important in your social and relationship order. As I write this about your auric energy I notice that your blue color is becoming violet (opening up with unconditional clarity) and is very charged, that your spiritual energy is amazed with what you are reading. As I go on, you are a man of convincing words, as well a composer of creative musical quality (you like to speak, sing, and you like music). This ability allows you to have good listening skills as well being responsible on many levels toward your goals. The loneliness that I see is that you are tired on many levels, that you have to be responsible for many of your friends karmic energy but you feel that this is your way that you show love, by carrying karmic issues on your associate's karma on their behalf. You hope that they would carry on themselves in the long run, but instead they have expected you always to do that for them now which you are very disappointed with inside because you did it out of love. But you didn't want to make a career out of this, because you want them to know that you care which is why you did it. Now is hard to get out because they have defined you as a carrier of their karmic pattern and expected you in this mind set to help them always. That is how they see you and you are not truly happy with this version of reality, but you feel sympathy and realize "why stop now", and so be it. Now you yourself are tired because when you need someone toward your side to freely give you energy and attention, when you are victimized on some level, there is no one who would come to your side freely except with a prize, that is a karmic debt, so you feel lonely that no one will take the time to listen to your drama and life lessons and difficulty (take turns), that no one feels what you are about, that you have feelings that they don't know how to care for you as you know how to care for them. So, you feel unfair treatment in these many relationships. That is why you feel the loneliness inside (know you need to be healed), it is like you are talking to deaf ears most of the time that no one can read your feelings and heart's expression even if you have communication with the ones whom you have relationship with, you still feel unfair energy from them because they don't see that you are human and have a heart, not subservient. So every time you talk to them it is like it is not talking or interaction on a common level, but an exploitation for favors and services, so this kind of energy interaction has now made you tired on many levels so you want to sing a song or write a poem to release your feelings so that you can be balanced. But me and the guardians hear you and understand your life experience and situation, know that you will be just fine. You have all the answers and you understand yourself. To further elaborate, I just want to say that there is this green mixed with the blue, well, we know that you support peace in your thinking and in your habits. You feel that you are the healer and who can do much to help heal the many relationships around you. But of the three persons who I mentioned earlier in your aura, I show that one of them has died (relationship disconnection or contract is over with). We see a discord of the relationship cords in your field, so it is very sad for you and these three beings because they all know each other and have relationships with you. The death of this relationship is like the relationship with you and them has come to an abrupt end and it hurts all parties. The way it ended was on a emotional difficulty for all sides, so there was a sense of sadness and hidden feelings among the party that is involved (and need to be expressed so healing can begin). So much healing that is needed, and much love and time is needed over here in this area of your life so your heart and emotional reality will be shut down for a while in relation to the relationship, until some kind of new contract is made for the old relationship contract has come to a quick end. I Kosol and the guardians know this will be your difficult time, but you are spiritual and I know you will heal and will move on. Yes it hurts, and yes there will be many tears, but you are a strong person. Cry you must, hate if you must, but in the end you are love and will always be that. Dear heart, we hope that your heart will heal more and more after reading our aura expression of you.

Example #4

Well, Dorothy, here is your aura. The color of your fields is red with blue, pink, and green. Also there seems to be green coming from a white light of star, coming and connecting with your heart cords. That white star is on the right side of your shoulder so it's related to a male person who is very spiritual in nature. Ok let's begin. The red that is associated with you is very hard and dark. Whenever this happens to a person, your life has been patterned toward preserving an object or idea. That means you live in a fixed pattern and it is very hard to change even if you want to. This was taught by your upbringing, so you owe much of this pattern to your cultural surroundings. You are not much a connected person to other human beings. You are more of a loner in your travels throughout life, a few friends and that is it. But you do have a public life in relation to spirituality and stuff because you are opened in this area all through you shine. Only interrelation to the spiritual worlds, other than that, you remain hidden in the silence. Only your few friends notice you, not other people. Now as for the blue, this blue is not of earth blue. It more related to keeping secret some higher knowledge, so this means that people can entrust you with personal or group secrets because of your unsuspicious character. So you are a good knowledge keeper. I am getting different vibration readings from you. There is a person standing near you, it is like an astral light being, his name is Ariel. He said he is one of your friends that you know of. He influences your life in many fashions both physically and spiritually as well as coming into your dreams to teach you things. He is green in color and pink, he said he have a very personal dedication to your existence and in many lifetimes just like this. He always walks with you. He wants me to tell you hi and as well that he is real and active in your life and not to be afraid. So the blue is related to Ariel, as well with several other light beings. Interesting, so he guides you in your speech, although is always to the point. Now as for this pink and green, well this is admiration from other lifetimes towards you in this lifetime, so in a way you have lots of memories and realistic connections toward other influences from other lives. Just know that Ariel is here to help you heal some of that lifetime, that you are not satisfied with throughout this lifetime. That's why your friendships with many people is not in abundance, and the people that you have relationships with now are your brother and sister from other lifetimes that are here to assist you along with Ariel, your friends, guides, and his support teams. So don't feel bad if you don't have lots of friends, it just that you have chosen this way. Only when you feel that you want more connections to other human beings, then your cord will change and you will have connection to more human beings so this can uplift you. The green is coming from the star that is related to Ariel's influence on your life. Somehow this is a very good thing, so you have yourself a person very dedicated to you. A long term friend in many lifetimes, he is an old friend and common guardian angel and is all-good. Well this is what I have to say right now.

Example #5

Ok beloved how are you doing? To begin beloved, let me said congratulations. You are going through an abundant positive experience at the moment. Your aura is very bright green and orange. There is a bright silver ball at the left side of your head, (don't want to say that you just inherited a baby, but is a similar kind of experience). As well there is red and blue and pink at the right. Ok, to begin the bright orange represents emotion of positive joy as well that you have accomplished a desired goal during this time. You are celebrating the new journey that you are in and also saying good bye to the old journey. Now as for the left ball, that is representing a break in your current relationship from your perception as a girl. That means dear heart you are venturing into the personal goal that you set out to accomplish and you are temporarily postponing your short term desire and now you are following your life term desire instead (you are now a women fully and no longer a girl), and guess what, you have friends who also support you in this. Like your parental units, both father /mother energy is strong in supporting your decision. Beloved there is also a concern for your well being. We know like you know, there is some difficulty that you have had in the physical form that can sometimes hinder you in many ways. I'm not saying that you have a weak lung or heart, but this hindrance is related to emotion. That means you can be over trusting of someone and thus sometimes disappointed because that person you trust sometimes, when you need him/her the most they don't show up all the time and thus you feel kind of disappointed and frustrated. Sometimes you want to tell them that, but you know like they pick up from you, that they know you are upset with them, so it's not your fault or reality's fault that this happened. It's just that they tried and that is what counts, so it is all good. Beloved, since you have green orange, this green is of the heart. That means you spent time a lot with nature and also with friends who enjoy the same peaceful scenery. So you go out to the mountains a lot. That is good beloved, and you are very careful about your diet all the time and what you put into your form as well. You enjoy natural herbs which means taking herbal vitamins. You enjoy being health conscious. Now you may have a lot of understanding of many types of knowledge, but you truly do feel alone because you want love and to have a family of your own. You are looking for compatibility with some of your current friends, but no luck yet. You are trying those that know what counts, and yes you want a partner, (is NICK THE ONE?). That nick, he is too much power. Oh well, that is just our 2-cents. Ok back to your story. Now as for the baby, we see that you have a baby. This is a relationship that you have and thus have given birth to this horizon. So from here on out it will be a new and also very interesting adventure, now you are not alone. Now as for the red, blue, pink on the right side, what this means is that it is related to a guy. That you find him very attractive in form and you have emotional trust in him. Before you didn't have this kind of experience with this person but now you do. It feels totally that this being is the one for you and you for him so you feel the need to be with him always and as well, he now reminds you of your father energy. So you have concluded that he is your soul mate or twin flame in this lifetime. You wish to be with him and it is all-good. We now take our leave beloved, be well.

Example # 6

Dear heaven one, I have so much to tell you. Your aura is full of symmetric symbols like formulas and code, and the color of your fields is hyper white, yellow, and tans. Here is where we see you standing near a field or plateau as well. There are ion storm clouds above you (these ion clouds mean to conceal your true reality from the environment as well, it's like to conceal your secret knowledge and identity, to only show people when the right time comes). In this assessment it seems that you are engaging in a task of discovery in relation to symbols and geometric designs of some sort. Dear one, now I go into detail of explanation of your fields and what it means. The symmetric symbols is relating to the understanding of science knowledge, as well as able to be organized in your structure and thinking. Dear one, you are a phenomenon within yourself. The formulas and codes, that is your ability to understand hidden basics within a complex pattern. That is why you are so emotional and so logical in attuning to simple solutions for a complex situation. Furthermore, as well, I see loneliness in your fields. It seems that you believe that you are in a classed mind of your own. Be well dear heart that you are not. There are others who are like minded and structured just like you on this planet and also very advanced as well. So you are not alone in the classroom which you have chosen. Now beloved for the hyper white meaning. It means total grasp or understanding of events and different views of reality. So you see, all is good from the multiple perspectives from where you have operated from. So to you nothing is really bad. For you each is a compliment to the same solution or desired goals that you have chosen. Now as for the yellow, well it is related to you for a craving of inspiration as well as complex thinking. Furthermore you have a great need and desire to eat tasty food, and also your metabolism rate is very high indeed because of your aura fields is large and vibrates high on the universal octave. As for the tans, that is related to rocks. However dear one your element is metal and rock, that is what makes you feel at home is in stone buildings and rocky deserts. So a castle would be a happy place for you, like in Ireland. Now as for the plateau, that is related to contact with off world inhabitants like alien vibrations and angelic life forms. Dear one, to sum your fields up, you are well. There is nothing unbalancing in your health or relationship to self or others. Further more beloved, you are changing in your cellular structure from a 2 helix to a twelve helix. Be well, be loved, and you will find the solutions to your current needs, in due time. For now dear one just enjoy your time off, or just be at peace... p.s. happy telepathic communication with the others... have fun dear one.

Example #7

Dear heart, you have a very interesting auric field. Your connection with the celestial worlds is strong. Your auric color is very gold/orange, plus there seems to be a silver/pink on your right side, that is like a pathway to another reality. Dear heart you have a very strong connection toward wisdom since you are full of curiosity and you have the ability to recognize medicines like a naturalist in herbs. Now as for the celestial, well beloved, what this means is it is related to another off world civilization that you come from and connect to. You belong to the monkey humanoids from the star system of the Scorpio constellation. The monkey people or humanoid beings are very well known for their ability in understanding dimensional travels. They have the ability to invent advanced medical technology. Their ships range from planet size to 6,000 mile long and 3,000 mile wide. That mean dear heart you understand the common sense of how people feel and what they need, so you have a highly developed nurturing motherly intuition of yourself and others. Beloved, many times when you run in to people you already have a sense of what condition of a karmic journey they are in, and already know how to approach them in a proper manner. Beloved you have the ability to calm people in an amazing way and especially in a crisis. You know how to bring organization to people or groups into a structure and show them the common good for both sides. Beloved, you are a naturalist in the people's areas. Also beloved you have a sense that somehow that you have failed in many of your desired goals. Well beloved that is not the truth because some of the events that you encountered are not coming from your chosen reality, it was inherited from some other group reality and the karmic lessons belong to them. It is just that you were put into something that you weren't ready for and thus everything seems to go wrong. Beloved don't blame this failed event on yourself, remember you inherited it not with your full agreement of free will. Beloved let it go, and do what is balanced as you have been trained for, every obstacle is an opportunity to grow, forgive, and move on, otherwise you yourself will need to be healed. Beloved there is also many young souls that seem to appear and disappear around you. What this means beloved is that when you have a group or individual soul that come to you, you have ways of assisting them, and with that they can move on and thus they will return in a later date to accommodate you in your journey as an appreciated thank you from their heart for guiding them in their journey toward their full potential. That means beloved that you have friends in many areas of your life. I know that you have love for music as well as for artistry. But gifts are another thing to touch on. It is a very beautiful art from your perception because of the challenge that it presents. Now beloved that you know that you are from another star system, some of your natural ability is come from your past existence on other worlds that you have brought with you to this earth civilization as a gift to raise humanity vibration's and consciousness. You know that you are a star child. The gold orange means you feel passion and understanding of every event. You love philosophy and in many cases you love to solve complex problems that you find challenging and you love to work with different team members and exchange understanding of the same common goals. You love to contribute back to your surrounding environment. Dear heart, you have a desire to be content with whatever you have, but you also long for yourself to be happy in all that you do and sometimes it's hard because of the lack of support from the atmosphere that you have been existing in. So in other words dear heart you feel the need of a friend to talk to most of the time, and that is okay. Now as for the silver pink, that means you have lived a double life, meaning you look normal on the outside but behind the scene you also have many things that you have to do for the world and surrounding atmosphere. That means you are doing your part to make this planet a better place to live for the future generation by raising it vibrations, and it is all good. I know beloved, now I see a blond women with green blue eyes, she is like someone close to you and she looks very traditional. This being you owe a great deal of admiration to because she was there for you when you needed someone to be with you. Now you owe it to her to do to her good in many ways, because this being is your best of friends from your life point of view. Now you are balancing the karmic debt that this being has bestowed on you, so you are doing a lot of cherished deeds from your heart in order to bring the karmic debt back to balance and you are enjoying it. You will be merry to this one soul so either way it goes, it all will be good. Dear heart be well, we now take our leave. Beloved, be well.

Example #8

Dear one yes your aura is reddish with blue on the right shoulder. Much work needed on the father and son relationship side. Wow, dear heart let's begin. Yes you are very busy, busy, and more busy. There is not much room in your life for a new journey at the moment, but you have made a promise toward one of your loved ones that you will make time for him. You can't put it to the side because it is your son, or best friend. Any way, you have made a commitment to this person, and I am sure you will fulfill it. Remember, it is hard to back out of it now. You have already given your word, so no matter what you must be there or your future in this relationship will not look too bright if you don't fulfill it. On the emotional level you are very active. Also you work with people throughout your actions. You are not a man of a lot of words but with documentation, you expect that from everyone. Now the universe expects that from you also. Is time for you to stand and show your worth to yourself, and as well you know how to help commit people to many obligations but now it's time to commit yourself to your personal obligation because you never make time for your personal life on the recreational level. So it is time for you to share love with yourself. Also it is time to bring other parts of your self into balance especially your family life and with your spouse. They need you more then ever now, so it is time to replace your busy schedule life with personal life also (to bring balance). To bring you personal enjoyment and happiness, you always please people on the public level. Now is time to please your inner circle also, as to give them time in your life as well. You will experience much health difficulty in your physicality due to feelings of loneliness in side your emotional life and have to take many medications for certain symptom that have arrived in your life, but all will be lifted with some uplifting happiness and laughter from spending some time with your family, especially your children. They bring much joy to you. It is good to be busy but not to the point you don't feel happy anymore. You know your heart and you know your limitations, don't ignore it anymore. You can't live without your family or their love for you. Your happiness is karmically bonded to them so take some pressure off, and schedule some time to be with them. It is best that way, life is short. Just do it and you will be rewarded from the guardians and family angels around you. It is all about sharing love.

Example #9

Hello dear one, I know you are doing fine on many levels. Well shall we begin your aura reading? Ah you don't need to answer we already know what you going to say, so let's begin. Hmmm, dear one, there is much to tell you. Your aura is very diversified with red as the primary color that represents very closely to your physical. As well your dormant color is brown orange (emotion and nature). There is picture of symbolism, that of a female, with blonde hair wearing a pink and white robe (shows understanding and clarity). She is surrounded with a blue colored atmosphere (inspiration toward responsibility), and on her head is a crown of daisy flowers (simple and pleasant in habit). She is also holding a pink rose (a healing gift, also nurturing children) this symbolism is very strong in your auric fields. Ok now dear one I am going to use light language to read your aura for you. Whenever your field shows diversity, that means you are in a search, or looking for some part of you that is missing that needs to recover in order for you to find peace of mind and of body. You are trying to find people of your type and like mind to share with each other love on your level of understanding and experience. As well the red that is close to your body, meaning healing, you are worried a lot about your health and also concerned of how to maintain your physical health. The color of brownish orange is very critical, at this time your life is in a struggling state of well beings. You have to take herbs and vitamin to help you feel better. As well you are trying to accomplish a certain desired physical goal in how you look, like you are trying to watch your diet. The symbolism of female that is shown in your aura, is the love that you have for the guardian angels and nature spirits that you have relationships with. It also shows how much you love your father since it is in the right side that your love and acknowledgment of the love that is from your dad is very strong. You are daddy's little girls on many levels. You feel admiration for your father a lot. The blue field surrounding the female figure shows you want children and to always give them full attention to their well beings. The flower in her hand shows that you have gifts in herbal understanding and love science and musical instruments and song. The blond hair and crown flower shows you appreciate everyone's beautifulness that is inside of them no matter what origin are they from. You don't feel there is a difference in people, in that you only see that they are creatures of mother /father God and need love just like you need love. Although you can never help people to the fullest you always do your best in praying for them and always tell them that they are not alone and that God is with them and that the angels are watching them. On many levels you have given them inspiration to continue on their chosen journey. As for now be careful about your health, and don't stress yourself too much on how you look for everything is a gift. Your heart is strong, but yet you need also to be inspired from your peers. It is time for them to acknowledge of how much you love them and they love you.

Example # 10 (This actually an Aura reading done on me, by my friend Liz in March of 2001)

My gift to you, my friend, from Liz (3/01)

First, my friend, as I enter your vibration I give to you your cosmic gift in order for you to enter the completion of your destiny. This vibration is a constant in your life and represents the gifts you are given to accomplish your mission and destiny including all that has been bestowed upon you. "Your cup runneth over" is what I see. You have an abundance of love. You are also offered all the pleasures of the world in abundance. Your vibration carries with it divine help and protection. You are extremely versatile because you can reflect the inspirations you receive, see, and feel. You can translate concepts into reality. You radiate the elements that are valued to you the most. In other words, if you do not see something as important you let it go (you probably drove your teachers crazy). You could've excelled in anything, but you only chose those you deemed important enough to carry on. Thus you radiate the most love, faith, and enthusiasm. You have the courage to tackle anything because you know you have success. Inspiration and energy are combined to give you quick and satisfactory results. You are a pioneer at heart and tend to enjoy change, (There is no fear for you) and you love to travel whether it is from an agreement or to fulfill an obligation. So on the materialistic side of things you must be careful not to overindulge your senses where you enjoy the many pleasures of material living. Otherwise, love, happiness, and success follow you. On the spiritual side your cup is also overflowing. There is a beautiful white dove above you that represents peace, truth, and the Holy Spirit. This all represents that when we give of ourselves and our spiritual gifts we create an unending supply of love. Your spirit is also in the hands of the guardians or the Hand of God from which cosmic inspiration flows. From here you quench the thirst for Divine Power. And speaking of power you are now entering into your most powerful years. Say goodbye to your youth. Use your talents toward useful goals and you will achieve your wildest dreams. You must balance the scales of justice and freedom. You must balance the scales of spiritual and physical realities.

This vibration you live under will lead you to honor provided you make every step of the way constructive and in the right direction (you can sometimes be headstrong and hasty which you must guard against) If others oppose you or your ideas be careful not to allow the difference of opinions to generate into quarrels. For that is what it is, just a difference of opinion. Remember my friend, you are a reflection, your divine power and eagerness to help others is inspirational and is wisdom to those who seek and want to learn. For there are those to who do not want their reflection known, not even to themselves.

You are loyal and passionate and therefore you enjoy marriage. You will provide a wonderful and happy family life to those around you. Love and peace is yours at hand. Now as I leave your vibration I see your aura, it permeates iridescent sparkles. These divine sparks of creation are all around you. You are a co-creator. And as I step back I see golden rings around you, like you would see in the ages of a tree. Each ring represents a great achievement. Now you are representing this tree of knowledge, providing support and building foundations. I also see a calendar and two wedding bands coming together for you. I have asked when will they be joined, or how long before they come together. They tell me on the calendar that we will know "for sure" in two months time! We are getting close to the time of joining in on this celebration. And last, your wife's aura is a radiant blue with green and pink flowing within and throughout in such a motion that it adorns her. All her inner beliefs and traditional qualities are based on the love you both share. Very lovely. I leave you now, in peace, my friend.

Example 11:

Kid Krayon-11/27/00

well, your aura is definitely, green and bright gold crytalline, with a lot of guides from the celestial realm accompanying you a lot...it look also there is a fracture in one of your relationship orbs on your right side, behinds you, and you definitely need healing here, or forgiveness to this loved one that it appear to be trapped in your fields... much love is radiated from you at the solar plex chakras (thirds chakras), ok there also the orbs, this are the orbs of relationship, since you have a clear organization of it... and definitely healthy, except for one of them, you have totally 6 relationships orbs,, with different color, the 3 of them is green, and the other is mixed multicolor, as you already know, one is located behind you on the right side, the other green is at your left side near the shoulder blaze area, the other is on the top left side of your bodys, near the crowns, the other is at the lower waste at the front, one is at the legs it alternate left and rights... and other is under your feet. is like a cushion of some sort... (that what it act like... like a rescue bubble)... ok lets begins...now the green part mean, you are a relationship beings in your aspects, you like to be connected, that how you learn about your self, you allow other to reflect your inner knowness, you don't actually know yourself in a fully conscouis way, so you know you need, other to help you to bring your knowledge into conscious mode... so every persons you come into contact to, they help to revise some of your memory of your self, so you love and enjoys company of many sorts... but there is also a injury in your relationship, that you experience with a closed friends for a long time... is the injured relationship orbs... behinds, you near your heart chakras. is on the left side so it means your feeling is hurt also, from this interaction with this love, one, it look like a female energy... (i hope it not your mother or some sorts), well much needed healing and energy of forgiveness from both party, that needed to be expressed and experience so both can be healed... well as for the bright gold crystallines, this is related to super powers and off worlds contacts, well you all ready know you have plenty of guides (light beings) to hang out with... except your energy is very high in vibration is like you are currently working on a project of some sorts. and are very intense at it... you know it coming up and you are about to be complete on its... it just there is some bugs to work outs, then your project journeys will be complete with your universal expectations... as i may see there is charisma and you burn lots of energy, you sure need food energy and meditation, to help your body to ground to this worlds, other wise you will ascends, into the other realm (fifth dimensional reality) so is all goods...and as for your guides, well you are in contact with a lot of them, they appear to be from the celestial realm, due to theirs cobelts colors of their fields, so as you may know, vivid dream and astral projection is of your liking as well as telepathic communication...so you have a lot of energy bless, well that goods...well as for the relationship orbs on your left side, this mean a students of your, so you have a person that you dearly love and are assistance in this person development in many area of her life, and you wish the best for this beings because she is under your physical and spiritual care ships... so is all good, because you feel like you and her are a family of many life time... (a sister of some sorts of feeling) as for the orbes of the at the solar plus chakras well this relate to strong guts feeling, you have plenty of that except that there is burning of energy, meaning you attract friends that this help you to be balance because they radiated calmness to your fields so every where you go, you always have friends with you... so to speak, because, the many friends help ground you and your energy... so you won't float away... (ascend mode) and as for the orbs at your feet, meaning you got support and protection from many sources. so you have friends or family in many areas of your fields, so you are not alone... and as for the orbs on your left side near the crown, this is related to female guides, that you have very vivid relation ship with... (a teacher of the light in female forms) grand mother figure... as for the for the orbs at the waste areas that relate to senshavel need, you feel that you also need love from everyone from time to time... it is a parent love, and love from a friends,, because even you sometime feel lonely... as the orbs at the legs is help you got leason friends this are friends that do things for you, you got both male and female one, ways to go...ok that it from me what is my grade?

Example 12:

well, jude, i have much to tell you about your auric fields, first of all, i want to tell you, that there is much scenery in your fields, is like you have many recorded memory and connection feelings to many place and some how have a sacred, feeling to each one of them... and all of this places does give you refreshed energy of courage and earth attuning feeling to your surroundings... ok, your aruric fields is very red, and plus yellow, orange, along with blue pink, well the most important part is there is a light beings, look like fairy to me... but big about 14 feet similar to the guardians height of 15 - 16 feet high... well ok, enough of my bull corning let's get started ok, here we go... the red color will this related to busy ness, you are in a adventure quests of energies connectiveness that is related to earths and medicine of the minds for health and answer reasoning, so your physical life can have more form and more sacred admiration in it and on your surroundings,,., so you pretty much are attuned to natures and healths, you love how you feel in the morning and how you are before you go to sleep, you are very attuned to the earth energies... and it geometrical creativity... so different scenery will energize your minds and body feelings... mountains, and water fall, is the sound and the mysterious of the cosmos, like rains and oceans scenery with pyramid shape objects etc...well, the yellow orange is this is related to feeling of connected to a thought, so you are pretty much a vivid imagery person that mean you can bright ideas in to reality, from visual in to art of drawing and sculpture, so you have artistic talents and can project them into physical forms from your minds of thoughts...

that is goods... a visionary...and as for the orange this also related to your struggle of every day life, there is a fight many time among you surrounding, because the energy of a certain place drain you, so you have to fight with your self to stay or not to stay? to help or not to helps? because you feel the need to be at a certain place and assist those who need you, but at the same times you know your energy patterns and also know your limitation of your ability and skill and you respect that ... so it hard, in that perspective for you...well as for the blue and pinks this is relate to channeling you have developed the gift to communion with other many vibration of light spectrum of realities... the blue is the ability to speak truth of what you experience and pink is the ability to listen to the hearts of the matter, to say what you experiences... well as for the fairys lights beings, that your nature guides, you are connect to the elementals fairy kingdom, flowers of many colors and fruits is your likings... well you do have sacreds feeling for everything that you touch and see, i admire that...so the light beings fairy is always leading you to sacred geometrical surrounding of some sort, they also walk with you in your dream a lot of times and they also show you herbs and medical herbs for healing and also methods of advance meditations to help other and yourself so you are not alones in your adventurous journeys... that is all goods, now what is my grade?

Jude Thursday, 11/23/00, 6:17 AM Hi, thanx for sharing this very kool site. Glad UR a TruthZone member. Maybe some night, you could drop the chatroom and meet some TZ members. Let the Auras shine! In Light, peace joy, Jude From: moderator of the TruthZone Web Site: TruthZone E-mail: jude2000@truthzone.net Can we post your reading on this site? ok

Example: 13

Andrea 11/28

so here you are again, ok, ready for your update, on your aura, ok lets, get with it... ok your auric fields is mostly yellow with green white, there seem to be a overwhelming event and responsibility that you have to take on, and can be very stressful and challenging...ok, it look like a big green balloon right near and on you 5 th chakras...and is very large, in deed, is like everything will be put on you, to handle, now here we go, this yellow is very intense, meaning you are being prepared mentally and feeling for this upcoming events or challenges... so your neck area will feel tire, and heavy, by appearance there seems to be light beings who is doing some kinds of fixing on your back and neck chakras is like they are taking something out look like colors coded (multicolor) crystals of some sort and putting in some very golden (multicolor) colored crystals,, what ever you are prepared for is look very important in your life lesson and journeys... so your will power are now increased along with mental function (linearly speaking) now for the white it mean clarity... ok, so you are doing your best to keep your minds field clear of everything... that goods... because is you will need it... in the long run of this coming up challenging journeys... now as for the green color that is heart, so lots of love will be needed and your fields is radiating lots of it during this stage... now as for the big balloons that will be a surprise, next three weeks you will have another updates... ok, what is my up date grade?

Anreas Thursday, 11/23/00, 8:26 AM Just another starseed from Cyprus saying "Hey I'm here". The time is fast approaching...be patient people. From: Cyprus E-mail: andre@spidernet.com.cy Can we post your reading on this site? dunno what u mean yet, but sure...

Example 14:

Sascha 12/1/00

hello, how are you? ok here your aura, the color is blue, but is a unstable blue, green, plus white, with a greendiss ball the size of a tire of a car, on your right side (above), there is redish on your hearts like you been into situation that you can't for gets,, it related to some one you care pretty much about, but, it appear that this same person, stabbed (meaning betrayed) you (but you know, it wasn't their fault, someone forced them to, to do that), and was taken a way from you... so the pain never truly heals... you still feel unconditional, love for this beings, but with bitter memory as well, so you feel confused and can not take a step forward or back wards, is like you are trapped, in many fashion, you still feel traumatic shock,, and wishes things can be different in relation to this person... but heavy feeling, things has already happen so you can only hide the pains, you scare to lets it go. because is hard to feel love again on this levels, but this love that you feels is no longer pure in forms, is mixed, with pain, and bitterness memories... so you want to forgets, is that just you can't for some unknown reason. this beings that you feel for, in your hearts, half of the way you forgive, you know that someone is behinds all of this game, that you and this person are in, and you want to know who is pulling the dirty strings... all you want is just, some one to return true love to you, the love that you sent out... because you are tire of waiting and wondering, who can be trusted, and who can not... you wish things were a little bits simpler, you don't minds all of this minds game, but at least, someone need to be fairs,, when fairs is necessary and needed at times, from time to time...ok as for the blue, that related to your connect to responsibility, it appeared to be unstable, meaning you have begun to feel lost of trust, to your surrounding in many way, even close friends is looking like foes,, you feel the need to be a lone,, and want to feel, your self to figure out, what is going on inside you... you are in a overwhelmed state, and wishes to feel valnarable for a week or too with out someone judging you. so you can be you childish and silly creative self,, with out worrying who is looking at you, and wondering what are they thinks about you... bad or good...so you needed to feel, love from a parent relationship friends... just to cry, and let's them know you may be, this or that, but even you have weakness, that is your strength, you are a tender hearted beings, you enjoy given love to those who, here for you and be audience of supports (you love fairness),, you don't enjoy being judged bad and good, but you love being told the truth even if your feeling is hurt along the process,, either way, it go, you always maintained a character of professionalism, is only a act to hide your true emotions, because you have a very tender heart, and cry a lot, if everyone know the true innocent child that you are, then they would love you all the time,, but at the same, time you are scare to let them know that, because you know reality, and you have trusted some one, and has lets them know about your innocent child before but that person or groups of persons, have betrayed your trusted, and judged you... so you didn't feel good from that, experience, is not that you are close hearted, but you have become cautioned, in all of your journey and surroundings..., well as for the green, that relate to business, and opened heart to children you enjoys, being a round kids, and love to help them out in education, sport, as well, as a big brother watch and protector for them... you and children get along very well, also you love being around elder peoples, it allowed you to gain wisdom, and sympathy feeling that how you learned compassion... you are a dad boys or girls... as well you have the green thumbs... (for flowerings) well as for the white, is a spirituals, you have had miracles happening to you, that someone you know died, and some how you saw them again, and they came to your rescue in many occasion, in many forms... and thus, you are inspired, in about the spiritual realm, so your minds is very, attuned to sacred feeling, and have highly respect for, spiritual places and events... so you love to flow with the spiritual worlds, because it keep your minds clear, of unnecessary obstacles... and is all goods... well the blue green ball, is something that you are doing for yourself on a personal levels for a friends that have earned your respect, and have proven his loyalty to you... so you will give this person, a gift, as promised from you... when the time come, you will have it ready, and given him the gifts... so is all good... ok that all i have for now, so what is my grade?

Sascha Thursday, 11/23/00, 1:30 PM From: Las Vegas Nv. E-mail: drdee23@hotmail.com Can we post your reading on this site? yes

Example 15:

Retha Rutherford
Thursday, 11/23/00, 3:00 PM

I am very interested in this Aura information. Regards Rusty
(Retha Rutherford

Web Site:
Rusty's Retreat

E-mail:
rusty@mountain.net

Can we post your reading on this site? yes

Well, Retha, I have much to tell you. As you may know I did
your aura before, but it was audio voice mail, and you are
familiar with you the colors of your field already. Now for the
update, your blue color is dominate now, but there is a new
formation of color that is materializing in your fields, it is the
violets color. Ok, this is interesting, when there is such a color
that means you have discovered a whole new talent that you
have, or didn't know about, this relates to the 6th chakras, so
don't be surprise if you began to become kind of psychical all of
the sudden. This is what is very much happening in your current
stage, but, however, there is much to work out in your field. It is
like there are secrets of your self that you need to work out, on a
personal basis. (Remember the orange color that is related to the
sexual encounter in your emotional field that needs to be cleared
or throw away, when you were younger). Ok, because your field
is being covered with a very dark blue color, those long
unconfronted parts of you will now begin to surface, and you
have a choice to let them go or forgive. Those events that happen
in you life as well as forgiving yourself so your new gift can
become fully used and developed. Now you have reached a new
level in your life, but it can't be a full filling one until you make
room in your heart for it. So you have to clear your self from the

unacknowledged past. That your update, and is all good...

Example 16:

hello, sindy juliano, ok i saw you at the website guess book... also,, ok let's begin.

hmm, something is wild about your fields... ok here is the color, oranges (high emotions and feelingly charged), in nearly all aspect, but there is a big, white bright crystals light balls (a gift that is being open, blessing and all that), that engulf your heart, heads, and upper part of your body... is like a totals, changes is happening in your life, thus come with it a new bright multi colors, this white colors is many, in spectrum so you will have new inspiration and challenges, but is a gifts from a friends that has give you this opportunity to expands, so great gratitude to this worthy friends of your, that believed in you, and has given you, a wild chance to prove your worth, and so you have, and thus, now you completed your present challenges and now are ready to move on, with a whole new out look, and creativity... ok the oranges here, meanings, there is some personals issue that you have to resolve, and good bye to the old, situation, that you have totally forgotten, but recently are now in your awareness again, it just a little, clean house of your feeling, so once you are done, you will have new room, for the new, excitement that you are anxious in getting in to... since is orange in all aspect, that mean you have many type of emotion, so, you feel very attached to nearly everyone that come into your path, passion, in other worlds,, once you have a challenges definitely, you are loyal to accomplishing the goals, so time, is nonexistent for you... as longs there is agreement, you have no problems in waiting, until the right moment to act, and full fill your distant goal, and you do it, with passion...now, there is a trouble, you have been living a life of some of your surrounding, and sometime is making you think that something is not right, about, such and such,, is true, it is not right, because don't you know you are being used, like a puppet, is ok to be used, only when, you know that you are, but in your case you don't know...so step back, and give yourself more love, and realize, that everything has a behind the scene agenda as well, you may thinks that you are doing goods, and are doing the things that you like, but look, again, who life are you living? your life or someone else?... i know you have great tied to love, one and friends and would do almost any thing on your level to help them or accompany them to some place when they asked your to, but you must know also you have individuality, and your self need, to have a personal time, for your self, even if you don't think you don't have time,, because, you must always have time for your self, for without self, there is no sindy juliano, do you understands?, passionate person...p.s. the crystal light ball, is changing you, as well, so you have complete your current learning lesson, and challenges,, you are now entering a new state of mind and life journeys... apparently there is healing that is being done on you, by both of the physical worlds beings and the spirituals worlds beings ... this light beings, look like doctor, of the physical reality and light beings of the celestial reality, they appear to doing healing on your body and many minds system, so are you in treatment for, some medical reason?, hmm, strange anyway, your aura is going through some amazing changes, as we speak, so you are becoming a powerful, beings, because your fields is growing brighter and brighter... well, this is it for now, what is my grade? oh yes you will get a up date in one month from now... reminds me...

Example 17:

Subject: Dorothy here your aura reading.

Well, Dorothy, here is your aura. The color of your fields is red, with blue, and pink green. Also there seem to be greens coming from a white light of star, coming and connecting with your heart cords. That white star is on the right side of your shoulder... so it related to a male person, who is very spiritual in nature...Ok let's begin... The red that is associated with you is very hard and dark. When ever this happen to a person, your life, has been patterned toward preserving of object and idea. That means you live in a fixed pattern, and is very hard to change, even if you want to. This was taught by your up raising, so you owe much of this pattern to your cultural surrounding, so you are not pretty much a connected person to other human being. You are more of a loner in your travel throughout life, a few friends that is it as well, now. But you do have public life in relation to spiritual and stuff, because you are opened in this area, all through you shine. Only interrelation to the spirituals worlds, other then that, you remain hidden in the silence, only your few friends notice you not other people. Now as for the blue, this blue is not of earth blue. It more related to keeping secret of some higher knowledge, so this means that people can entrust you with personal or group secrets, because of your unsuspicious character. So you are a good knowledge keeper. I am getting different vibrations reading from you, there is a person standing near you, is like astral light beings, his name is Ariels. He said he is one of your friends that you know of. He influences your life in many fashion both physical and spiritual, as well as coming into your dreams, and teach you things. He is green in color and pink, he said he have a very personal dedication to your existence and in many lifetimes just like this. He always walks with you. He wants me to tell you hi...and as well, that he is real and active in your life... and not to be afraid. So the blue is related to Ariels, as well with several other light beings. Interesting, so he guide you in your speech, although is always to the points. But that you thought. Now as for this pink and green, well this is admiration from other life time to you in this life time... so in a way, you have lots of memory and realistic connection toward other influences from other lives. just said that Ariels is here to help you heals some of that lifetime. That you are not satisfied with, throughout this life time, that why, your friendship with many people is not in abundance, and the people that you have relationship now, are your brother and sister from other life time that are here to assist you along with Ariel your friend guides and his support teams, so don't feel bad, if you don't have lots of friends, it just that you have chosen this way. only when you feel that you want more connection to other human beings, then your cord is changed and you will have connection to more human beings so this can more uplifted to you... and the green Coming from the star well that is related to Ariel's influence on your life, somehow, this is a very good things, so you have your self a very person dedicated to you a long life term in many life time, he is an old friends and commons guardians angels and is all-good, well This is what I have to say right now. So what is my grade?

Dorothy Kirton Thursday, 11/23/00, 5:19 PM I have no website. I am With the mediums. From: Myrtle Beach, South Carolina Web Site: I have No website E-mail: harleyk@n...

Example 18:

Subject: Connie aura update.

kosol: Well, hello Connie K., how are things this holiday season? Well let's begin your aura update, as you may know many things have materialized in much fashion since the day I did your first reading... Here's your aura. It is blue all over, and green on the right side near the shoulder and head area, hmm this look bad, the green color on the right means there is instability, is not clear, and have unformed feeling inside it. This is your decision making in your relationship to the male side, so it will be hard for you to act and make true decisions in this three month period. I will go further in details, for now let's concentrate on the blue. Well the blue color is a very clear and dominant field in your fields. It is related to caring for yourself and your responsibility to carry out your relationship with daily commitment. There is nothing wrong here, except for the green on the right side, this relates to a personal past situation which is coming back into your life and needs healing on it. Since it is green it relates to the heart, as well as a past relationship with a father figure, so is something you have to deal with, and need healing of... other wise it will affect your ability to make decisions in the long run of things. So your right side of your body will feel heavy and your mind on that side will feel crowded with thought also. There will be fear that will arise in your experience in relation to that relationship experience that you need to deal with... Now, everything else look ok, from my perspective, also I know you, that you will ask me for anther update, ok just post anther one. I'm having an introduction from your guide about your children or several persons that you have relationship with, like you are the mother to them and they are your offspring's. So there will be more on it later... ok That is it...

Connie K Thursday, 11/23/00, 5:21 PM The last reading you did for me was great... Call me greedy... but if you have time I would sure love another. Thank you so much. From: Manitoba, Canada E-mail: ckraeker@m... Can we post your reading on this site? sure

Example 19:

Karen's Aura

Kosol: Ah ha, hello Karen, it has been a long time since the Kosol you know and the guardians you know commmuned with you. My journey in the fifth has been enlightened, also while I was away, my other counter alter ego maintain the formation of my existence which he and his guardian has done well. OK enough about me so how are you doing? Are you disappointed with me? I know you have been, in a way, but still I have to give you a reflection. I know you love me very much and also hated me too. In a way, I guess there is a fine line between love and hate among friends...ok enough of our relationship on the Internet, let's do the readings... are you ready for this?

Kosol: I know you are, otherwise you would have removed your name from the aura reading list. OK, the color of your aura is very cobalt of blue (responsibility to other beings more than self) and tree red (health care awareness on self and other) as also yellow (mental and will power) and oranges (sensual of felling lonely and helpless sometime) now the cobalt blue is on the right side on top of the tree reds, this mean that someone in your family is going through a spiritual awakening, this person or so to seem your husband is having a total life restructuring, since is on the top of the reds that mean you on the other hand are helping physically of how to deal and emotionally of how to go through this. Is like you are grounding him and also counseling him, this is a very interesting event in your life, further more, there is also, this yellow it relate to thinking and acting, you have a lot of stress as well, because during this time you are experience a lot of mental and structure reintegration as well, so your emotional state is very unclear at this time of finding solution and solving different problems that seem to arises daily, so that mean you have to be alert a lot and have to use a lot of all the spear time you have, in order for you to deal and transform all of this arising event into opportunity ... for you and your family growing process... now the relation of tree, this mean,, herbal when ever this come up in the aura shape you can be sure that health conscious in the activity of your life as well as time management... so time to you is very precious... further to elaborate... the guardians on your behave have asked me to tell you, that everything with be rapid for you and your soul group at this time because of the photon effect on the earth... so a lot of your karmic pattern are coming to a close and time for you is erratic as well, fast and hasty... like everything is out of the expectant desired event... within your own understanding... be well... my Karen,, we are family of light... now you don't have to grade me, but how that I do OK or so so... now the most important things that is important to you is your immediate family member at this time,, so hang tight,, do what you know best be there for them as they would for you... take time also for your self, because you needed it... from you friend, Kosol ouch, sometime crazy, sometime silly, and sometime just out there... peace be with you... for you Karen update are required every time you needed...

Karen Thursday, 11/23/00, 6:23 PM

I'm interested in a reading!! Will you contact me for this? Thanks, much! Karen :)

From: Pennsylvania

Example 20:

Haley's Aura Reading

Kosol: Hello dear heart, how are you? Your aura is so blue and dominantly close to the body, (related to music and responsibility, as well as planner of activity) and above it there is the orange red (forgiveness of self and event, emotion). Now there is some issue going on that you need to transform into the light, it is in front of you, the color is yellow (mental will power), is like you have developed a karmic debt, related to the stomach and lower area, so if you have pain and injury at that area, well that is the result of many troubling patterns of events that lead you to the point of not trusting the spiritual self of innocence. It is like everything is hard for you in this area, especially in relationship to father figure. Furthermore, there is the son or grandson, looks very dark in complexion, that seem to raising it hand both of them, to be excepted in your life and love fields, tell me dear heart are suffering from some kind of illness in the area which I just previously mention? If you do, dear heart, don't be alarm it will pass, and will be uplifted, because of the earth changes, and the entering of our existence into the fourth dimensional reality during this time, what you think will materialize... be at peace dear heart, know that your spiritual brother and sister are with you in your journey every step of the way...now as for the kid at your left side. That is showing a renewal of your current belief structure. You are given a second chance to make things right, dear heart. know this, that second chance is hard to come by most of the time... now the blue is the call of higher responsibility (in this case to your self evolutionary process), as you could see, is close to your body. This also means that physical healing is being accelerated in your matrix of existence as well as unfinished karmic desires are leaving you. So it don't have to stress you anymore, dear heart... blue by it self in this case meaning that you have now becoming aware of life simpleness and it's preciousness, so every little thing now means a lot to your life pattern for you have awakened during this time, and also appreciated many event that you have encountered where before you think nothing of, but now, you understand it's significance since this blue has orange on top of it, meaning that you enjoying being passionate about activity, of your choice (doing something for everyone as a gift) and also it has red (earth and physical activity), this mean you like your surrounding environment and other people to complement your works and like to show off your CO-creative capability to friend and family... furthermore, these three colors are now changing also after you read my auric reading of you. As you can see, you have come along way in a short among of time as well you may have a voice to speak your desire through showing people love with action, but now, sometimes, it is also hard for you to forgive some situation, until some action of balance is acted on by the other party without you asking them too act on it, then forgiving is easy, except sometime, is hard because some of the party that you deal with, have no idea of how you feel and some of them just leave or gone without you being aware they have existed in your life stream (a sense of being left alone or betrayed), so therefore, you have a lot of karmic debt from the other party to, so they owe to you and to themselves to sometimes make things more balanced, just like the father figure of your life, come and go, without a lot of love interaction, and thus this leave you with a feeling of not trusting men, because of the hurt that you are afraid of will come into your life, as examples of past experiences show, and in the long run, this make you not complete in your life lesson. But now you are trying to rewrite this belief structure from this old past experience, because you feel that life is life and now that you understand that bad and good is working together to better you and your situation, so you are transforming your old belief system into a more natural order of the universe type of belief which 'give everyone a chance' to prove themselves that they are your friend or foe, should you stay or go? As you can see, everything's is now good... so how did I do?

Haley Thursday, 11/23/00, 9:17 PM

From: Florida
E-mail: haley4u@hotmail.com

Example 21:

Tammy's Aura

Kosol: Dear heart, how are you? Dear heart I know you are doing just as best as you can, and there is much more in your life that you will experience, so everything will be well, take heart dear beloved, that you are not alone in the journey that you have chosen to participate in.

Let's do a reflection of you. My goodness dear heart, there is much to tell you about your auric fields, there seem to be a silver blue light of many candling multicolor that seem to bestowing it present upon you (guide's and guidance from the cosmic family of light and love). On the background of this bestowed multicolor light (different individual beings with common interest and desire) is a star and space. Now as for your aura color, dear heart, there seems to be apparent that you have another individual in your field or life that mean you have guest in your life at this time from the journey of event ... your color is blue, green, and rosy red, well dear heart what this mean is very easy to describe to your matrix, the silver blue light is the light of guardian angels and hope, this is bestowed on you because you requested this from the heavenly order which they sent it to you as a give to show that you have many wonderful event ahead of you, and the sky is not the limit, the many star as the back ground meaning opportunity, or place where you will be going, with new friend and event will be on the midst of your life interaction during this time. As you will have known your creativity has risen many foes during this current time and forward into the future (result from the earth entering of the photonic belts). as well the silver light is meaning you have a spiritual friends, which is your two kids, your ex-husband, and your current one, they are your angels, as well... many gift is bestowed on you dear heart. now for the candle symbol this mean soul kindle, when this occur in your fields that mean you owed a blessing to a person, in other life time and they also owed a blessing to you,, this will careened you to again meet each other in other life time, in the future as friends or family relationship,, now for the space atmosphere that mean, clarity, now at this time dear heart you have some much clarity of your life, it just of how you show it, either way you see it, is all good, never dear heart were you confused, just surprised, but now you are well and balanced as well as clear so the future look very bright, and karmic owning is also dear hearth coming to a close during this time. now dear hearth the blue in your case it mean remembrance, so you dear heart have now become spiritual in your ritual habits, you have created a very sacred duty for your self during this time, and has become your self very sacred as well, and you also dear heart have been planning and acting to present your sacredness to the environment (the world at large), so that you can have a good sacred feedback. Dear heart, know this beloved we of the spiritual brother and sister honor your sacred duty to your beloved one and the choose which you show it to present... in your own uniqueness, now for the green is mean nature and heart beloved, your feeling for commonality has grown, you also, have evolved into a more full conscious of a beings... there fore dear heart you are at peace with all that is around you and with in you...the rosy red is admiration as well as falling in love to all, you have so much admiration for life during this time, so you love all and cherish all. to you dear heart everything is happiness even more...

Dear heart, to sum it all up, you have been through an uplifting event lately that it will forever change you, and it has, for the betterment of yourself, so as of now dear heart we see no unbalances within your matrix. You are complete and happy. PS: how is your website doing?

know this dear heart we love you very much... Unconditionally. Tammy Thursday, 11/23/00, 10:33 PM

Example 22:

Syllia's Aura

Kosol: Syllia Blake here your aura. Dear beloved there is a new energy emerging within you... Let us describe what is happening, currently dear heart your aura is orange and with surrounding different color orb, but, as the we can see, there is seem to be a walk-in of your new self overriding your current self, in other words dear heart your are ascending into a full conscious beings. Your new current aura is bright multi-gold color (multidimensional wisdom and DNA activation from a 2 to a 12 helix), dear one plus blue, and silver also... Dear heart currently you are currently experiencing of a lot of psychic phenomenon. In your currently life, on the miracle and transmutation side, now let's go deeper now...in this excellent issue... the past auric field is orange this mean that your emotion is very separated at this time while it being transmutated into other higher dimensional existent, so dear heart you will feel, a need for closeness with the one you feel a relationship with. Thus this is a time, well you dear heart will experience once again you are in a child like stage of the human development with some increase of new ability and transformation of old one into new one as well, so to tell you in lemon term, dear heart, new arising is in your midst, now the different color orb is the connection that you have with other group soul who, you seem to influence and they in turn influence you. Is like you dear heart are teaching and councilor to them and as for them they are your mirror of feedback. Dear heart during this journey of the new arising you will feel the need to rest a lot as well to be isolated many time from know atmosphere of many friends, because you will experience higher creativity that you have never experienced before, dear one... the multi-color orb that surrounds the edge of the auric fields is loosing up, so that mean you will no longer have companionship on that level, during this time of your transformation into higher beings... so be prepared to have less connection to people... Dear one, as well you will be advancing in channeling ability beloved so this is your gift to assist humanity to be able to relate the higher message of guidance for the current people that has not yet complete their own transformation. Dear one you should be honored that this gift is bestowed on to you, by the heavenly order.

Now beloved the new color of gold, blue, and silver, let's describe what this mean to you, gold beloved is very high in your case it means awakening from spiritual sleep, so dear heart expect a miracle venture in your life, because you will have infinite knowledge and wisdom that you can use as well you will be able to see guide and walk with higher beings on all dimensional existence... Don't be ashamed or afraid, for it is all good, beloved. You are not along in your journey.

Now the blue, beloved, as you may know, many souls will come to you automatically, so be prepare to nurture them on many level, your worlds, words, and responsibility will be sacred from now one to all soul along with the universe's. Have fun dear one.

Now as for the silver dear heart this is the ability to use psychic power, you will able to talk telepathic and see aura and understand the science of miracle... so be joyful that you will walk with the angels of the spiritual and the angels of the physical worlds. As we are all are angels, that is it from us dear heart, be at peace and joyful, that you are an elder soul...

Example 23:

Gloria's Aura

Kosol: Dear light how are you? Are you ready for your reflection? I know you are, OK dear heart shall we begin. Dear heart your aura is spacy with red and cosmic color, that mean dear one that your aura is being restructured for higher connection, as you may know, let us elaborate even further. The color of your field is red, pink, blue, and guardians white, now that's where you sit and look into the cosmos. That mean you are a specter of creation and life, so during this time you are in a learning journey of observation and not yet a participator.

Now the spacy means open minded, and cosmic colors mean nonjudgmental of attitude. You are in a way a creatively thinker and cheerer. Now this reconstruction of your energy fields toward higher connection meaning that the earth's entering of the photon belt and you are becoming a 12 helix. Dear heart the red color that is around your body is related to the desire that you want to full fill and are acting on it, which is to better your life and relationships to self and others. The red here is so pure, that mean you are doing good, to your self, you wish nothing more than peace and good on yourself and others. Now this red has connected to pink blue, that mean you love responsibility and carrying out duty and also love to socialize with caring friends as well as speak your innocent thoughts with creativity. Dear one, you have many gifts to offer the surrounding environment as well. You are a lover of the arts, and are attracted to paintings that bring inspiration of culture and music. You also have a serious side as well to your family, but all and all you are a teacher among the elite, and are loyal to the God force and the human spirit which is truth. Now as for as the guardians white, this means you have a connection with higher guidance from higher realm, dear one. Now as I can see, there is some issue also that you need to work out with those that depend on you, because this sometimes makes you feel overwhelmed, yes dear one we understand what you mean, because you are only one person, so sometimes you can 't be at too many place at once. Dear beloved what ever choices you make know this, your guardian angels are with you every step of the way. Now there is a green ball, at your left arm. Well, this means you have a lady or women that have guided you in many ways, but, now you wish to grow on your own, and in a way you wish and want to let the other beings of guidance know your thoughts without damaging the current relationship. So dear heart speak your desire and it shall be granted, know this friendship is forever, love and friendship are always real. Be well beloved, always we are your friends, from us Kosol and the guardians.

Example 24:

Heaven Xinli

Kosol: Dear heaven one, I have so much to tell you. Your aura is full of symmetric symbols, like formula and code, and the color of your fields is hyper white, yellow, and tans. Here is where we see you standing near a field of plato, (or plateau) as well. There is ion storm clouds above you (this ion cloud meaning to conceal your true reality from the environment as well, is like, to conceal of secret knowledge and identity, to only show people when the right time come). In this assessment it seems that you are engaging in a task of discovery in relation to symbol and geometric design of some sort, dear one, now I go into details in explanation of your fields, and what it means. The symmetric symbol is relating to understanding of science knowledge, as well as able to be organized in your structure and thinking. Dear one, you are a phenomenon within your self. The formula and code, that is your ability, is to understand hidden basics within a complex pattern. That is why you are so emotional and so logical in attuning to simple solutions for a complex situation. Furthermore, as well, I see loneliness in your fields. It seems that you believe that you are in a classed mind of your own. Be well dear heart you are not, there are others who are like minded and structured just like you on this planet and also very advanced as well. So you are not alone, in the classroom which you have chosen. Now beloved for the hyper white meaning. It means total grasp or understanding of events and different views of reality. So you see, all is good from the multi perspective from where you have operated from. So to you nothing is really bad. For you each is a compliment to the same solution or desired goals that you have chosen. Now as for the yellow, well it is related to you on a craving for inspiration as well as complex thinking. Further more you have a great need and desire to eat tasty food, and also your metabolism rate is very high, indeed, because of your aura fields is large and vibrates high on the universal octave. As for the tans, that is related to rocky, however dear one your element is metal and rock, that is why what makes you feel at home is in stone building and rocky desert. So a castle would be a happy place for you, like in Ireland. Now as for the plateo that is relate to contact with off world's inhabitant, like alien vibrations and angel life forms. Dear one, to sum your fields up, you are well, there is nothing unbalancing in your health or relationship, to self or other. Further more beloved, your are changing in your cellular structure from a 2 helix to a twelve helix. Be well, be loved, and you will find the solutions to your current needs, in due time. For now dear one just enjoy your time off, or just be at peace... p.s. happy telepathic communication with the other... have fun dear one.

Heaven Xinli Friday, 11/24/00, 5:48 PM I would be much appreciative of an aura assessment; please feel free to include anything... From: here and now E-mail: celestialamoeba@i-link-2.net

Example 25:

Steve from Milwaukee

Kosol: Hello dear heart, how are you doing? I know you are doing just lovely. Very well beloved, are you ready for your reflection? I know you are excited, and ready. OK dear heart here we go, beloved there is much to tell you about your auric fields. You have a lot of connection to nature as well also with the humanoid kingdom. What show on your fields is the ability to commune with animals as well as with your environment. Now hear this out beloved, what we see is the sky is moving fast, (the clouds that is across the sky moving rapidly across from one point to the next simultaneously) as you may know dear heart in this form I see what look like merman or a humanoid life forms, apparently is your energy. You are not of earth origin dear heart, you look really like amphibian (look like frog humanoid), one of the species that join the galactic federation family some 3.5 million year ago, so that mean you have the power to manipulate minds and also situations dear heart. You have the capability as

67

well as possessing the potential to be a master of psychology. You have much wisdom to offer this world beloved. Since you have a connection to the amphibian species, it appear that your presence of a being was sent here to incarnate and to gather information on this planet, also to help evolve them as well. You are not alone dear heart, there is a lot of your species of brother and sister here also. Now as for your aura dear heart it very from brown, to blue, to violet, as well as to green, as well as to orange, and finally shape shifting symbols. Dear heart you have also power to shape shift into or out of any situation and karmic lesson as well. Let's go into details of everything that we have already mentioned beloved.

Kosol: The sky moving fast, well dear heart what this means is that, to you, there is no such thing as boring, or time moving slow. You live accordingly with event, and as for you, only the event counts, and what you gain from it..

Kosol: Cloud moving across the sky rapidly, this means, dear heart, that event and karmic lesson cannot trap you or make you a victim of any fashion or form. It seems that you are immune to situations, and only situations that you desire to exist will exist, and the ones you don't will not exist. Dear heart you are a blessing from above to this planetary consciousness.

Kosol: The humanoid part dear heart is to show that you are from another world or star system, in other words dear one, you are a star child, newly arrived here to earth so earth is a new and exciting place for you to be here, as well as a good playground and learning center for you.

Kosol: Since you from other world, you also have brought your civilization's gift to this planet, that is the power of being master of psychology, that mean you have power to manipulate both people and environmental energy and psychological vibration and event toward the common good of all. So dear heart you have much wisdom to offer, because you can see what is true from a multidimensional point of perceptions. To let you know dear heart, go to my web site on earth section and click on Sheldon update, go to the main page of his web site to learn a little bit about your species, on the galactic federation members, your species is amphibian, frog like humanoids.

Kosol: Dear beloved since you can shape shift your color that mean dear heart that you can change personality to adapt to any situation, but with the same intention, to accomplish the desired goals. Now for the brown, that is related to understanding people and pattern, you are well knowledgeable with people and how they are operate. Blue means you understand the point of every learning lesson beloved, is like you can pick up on the hidden meaning, what is going on in a situation, what caused it, and what is the likely result as well what is the solution. Now to the violet, you see visions and you have the ability to put thought into people as well as to receive them as well. Telepathic communication. is your specialty. Green is the heart, that means you like simpleness but love technology and are into invention also to help the common good, so you feel every situation. You are a scientist of the heart and orange, this means that you have compassionate feeling for all that is uplifting and life giving and as well you have sympathy for those who suffer. In many event you are a lovable being just like all of your species member, you dear heart just like your fellow citizen of your worlds, caring unconditional love vibration. It is one of the traits of your species. Now as for the shape shift that means the ability to adapt quickly and at the same time maintain your objective goal, to accomplish it, for the better of all.

Dear heart we apologize for the long reading, but it was necessary, be well dear heart, know that we always love you, peace and light beloved.

STEVE Friday, 11/24/00, 7:27 PM YOUR SITE IS REFRESHINGLY NEW AND VERY

INFORMATIVE. YOU DID A GREAT JOB AND I PLAN TO VISIT HERE REGULARLY.

STEVE From: MILWAUKEE, WI.
E-mail: HALJORDAN2112@EXCITE.COM Can we post your
reading on this site? YES

Example 26:

Matt's Reading

Kosol: Dear heart, you have a very interesting auric field. Your
connection with the celestial worlds is strong, your auric color is
very gold orange, plus there seems to be a silver pink on your
right side, that is like a pathway to another reality. Dear heart
you have a very strong connection toward wiseness, since you
are full of curiosity and you have ability to recognize medicine
like a natural list in herb. Now as for the celestial, well beloved,
what this means is it is related to another off worlds civilizations
that you come from and connect to. You belong to the monkey
humanoid from the star system of Scorpio constellation, the
monkey people or humanoid beings are very well known for
their ability in understand dimensional travels as well. They have
the ability to invent advance medical technology. Their ships
range from planet size to 6,000 mile lone and 3,000 mile wide.
That mean dear heart you understand common sense of how
people feel and what they need, so you have a highly developed
nurturing mother intuition of self and other. Beloved many time
when you run in to people you already have a sense of what
condition of a karmic journey they are in already and know how
to approach them in a proper manner. Beloved you have ability
to calm people in an amazing way and especially in a crisis. You
know how to bring organization to people or groups into a
structure and show them the common good for both sides.
Beloved, you are a naturalist in the people's areas, yes also
beloved you have a sense that somehow that you have failed in
many of your desired goals. Well beloved that is not truth
because some of the event that you encounter is not coming from
your chosen reality, it was inherited from some other group
reality, and the karmic lessons belong to them. It is just that you

were put into something that you weren't ready for and thus everything seems to go wrong. Beloved don't blame this failed event on your self, remember you inherited it, not with your full agreement of free will. Beloved let it go, and do what is balance as you have been trained for, every obstacle is an opportunity to grow, forgive and move on other wise you yourself will need to be healed. Beloved there is also many young souls that seem to appear and disappear around you what this mean beloved that when you have a group or individual soul that come to you, where you have way of assisting them, and with that they can moved on, and thus they will return in a later date to accommodate you in your journey as an appreciated thank you from their heart for guiding them in their journey toward their full potential. That means beloved that you have friends in many areas of your life. I know that you have love for music as well as for artistry. But gift, is another things to touch on, it is a very beautiful art from your perception because of the challenge that it presents. Now beloved that you know that you are from other star system meaning some of your natural ability is come from your past existence on other worlds that you have brought with you to this earth civilization as a gift to raise humanity vibration's and consciousness, you know that you are a star child. The gold orange means you feel passion for understand of every event as well you love philosophy and in many cases you love to solve complex problems that you find challenging, and you love to work with different team members and exchange understanding of the same common goals. You love to contribute back to your surrounding environment. Dear heart, you have a desire to be content with whatever you have, but you also long for yourself to be happy in all that you do, and sometime is hard because of the lack of support from the atmosphere that you have been existing in. So in other words dear heart you feel the need of a friend to talk to, most of the time and that is OK beloved. Now as for the silver pink that mean you have live a double live, meaning you look normal on the outside but behind the scene you also have many things that you have to do for the world and surrounding atmosphere, that mean you are doing your part to make this planet a better place to live for the future generation, by raising it vibrations, and it is all good. I know beloved, now I see a blond women with green blue eye, she is like someone close to you, and she looks very traditional. This being you owe a great deal of admiration too because she was there for you when you needed someone to be with you. Now you owe it to her to do to her good in many ways, that this being is your best of friend from your life to life stand point of view. Now you are balancing the karmic debt that this beings has bestowed on you, so you are doing a lot of cherish deed from your heart in order to bring the karmic debt back to balance and you are enjoying it. You will be merry to this one soully so either way it goes, it all will be good. Dear heart be well, we now take our leave, selamut... Beloved, be well.

Matt Sunday, 11/26/00, 6:49 PM From: Tennessee E-mail: MattmanII@webtv.net

Can we post your reading on this site? yes

Example 27:

Patty's Reading

Kosol: Beloved I got so much to tell you, your aura is going through many difficulties during this time. Your color is so physically red, and there is a yellow green (this related to a person on the father side of polarity who you admire and love very much) ball with a silver blue cord connecting (a very dedicated relationship) to your heart chakras as well. There appears to be an angel near your side and is like you are going through a recovery of some sort, is like you are being counseled in many areas of your life. Beloved let us explain what is going on. When ever a person's aura is so red like this that means you are at this time, beloved, going through a test of karmic lesson, that means you will experience the worst fear of your life coming true, like right now it is related to being sick physically that you will have to overcome by riding it out. Know that this sickness is not of your causing but instead is from the father side of relationship. From beginning you always has the submission to follow someone you trust on the father relation but however that dependency is now being taking a way from you, as well, so for the first time you have to do things on your own, which you never had to before, you always had been taking care of by the party that loved you. So now that caretaker have move on to another existence, so there fore you are forced to be alone and this is not an accustomed feeling that you are used to, and thus it scares you, and so now that you have to mirror the most things that you are trying to avoid in your life which is to look out for yourself and well being. Beloved I want to let's you know that your angels are with you, your figure of father authority. Now as for the cords, you are looking for a similar relationship that your presently experienced before. That you have with the father figure to you, but you are scared that you will never find anyone or any party with that similar vibration and care taking attitude, so that is why you are feeling at lost and physically not balanced, beloved, know this is only temporary. The feeling and sad physical symptoms from this unexpected event will pass, then you will emerge from this misconception of life reality, so therefore dear heart all will be well. Now as for the cords, this represents a connection to the one that you lost, so their presence is still strong within you and around you (angel energy), but however, you did gain many hardships from this and also wisdom as well, to be able to stand on your own. We therefore, dear heart, salute you. Further more your symptoms of sadness will be uplifted. There is an angel of a person, also male who will come into your life and will be your new and uplifting sunshine, so beloved is all good all the way around. Don't be sad and don't thinks you are alone anymore for you are not. Now be happy and let things flow, or else we won't buy you an ice cream (just kidding). Oh well over all things, everything will be fine. OK dear heart is all good. Salamat gurin jirin.

Patty Sunday, 11/26/00, 6:51 PM From Can we post your reading on this site? sure

Example 28:

Mary Dunahue's Reading

Kosol: Hello dear heart how are you? I know you are doing fine, beloved. To begin with I want to say your aura is very appealing to us guardians. OK beloved let us say that you have many types of nature and devas types of auric fields. In this field I see, blue violet colors with tree brown, and many types of cords to many natural scenery as well as many type of animals. As you may know, I see wolf and eagle energy types that are very strong in your fields. Also I see totem pole, with a quili bear on top, then the eagle, then the wolf, then a plan, and then Egyptian symbols of the healing cross. Now dear hear let's explain what this all means to you. dear heart the many type of nature and devas type of auric fields meaning you connection to the environment and for it concern of a well being is strong. that mean beloved you have a gifted talent to understand land resource and how it should be used as well the history of a place and it many spiritual and life supporting value, and what energy and structure should go right there or here... Furthermore beloved, the realization that you have respect for nature is also a gift that you inherited from your great grand father, who also is attuned to the environment around him. My beloved I keep getting image of American Indian life style, and it traditional pattern projecting from your auric fields saying that you are a healer type of beings who has dimensional travel capability. I see you as this silver hair beings holding a golden phoenix feather, and there are two young persons who sit down in front of you, a boy and a girl who you are seemingly conveying star knowledge to. Dear heart I do understand what all of this means. It means beloved that the old meaning is your wise energy and the children are your son and daughter who will carry your legacy into the golden age of reality. The feather is what I call, a new begin and also the ascension of you and your reality has begun, you auric expression is going to be a very long one. now for the blue violet color, well that is related to spirituality. You are very gifted in that also, beloved. The violet is related to your sixth chakra, in this case you have awakening dream of astral projection as well as conscious one. The blue is what we call 'you have guide's in your world', meaning don't saying wrong or right things because everything you said come true, that is why you contain the gift of truth. So what you utter will materialize. Now for the tree brown that is oneness with peaceful feeling and the gift of understanding karmic balance, and their related solution. Now the many type cords that connect to the natural scenery is related to sacred sites, beloved it appear you have been all over the planet and as well to many holy energy sites. So many miracles you have performed and also have witnessed. Now as for the animal connection beloved this means different constellation, so you have a strong connection to the many constellations of heaven and it various dimensional realities. That means beloved you have a friend in higher realm looking out for your best interest and also your safety as well. You have higher friend here on earth as well. Now the wolf that related to your best friend he/she is always there by your side and also showing you to be careful in all things, the wolf energy is a person and personal best friend of you. Now as for the eagle, this is a female energy that is related to transcending. This being is also your best friend, it is a female being whom you have walked many journeys with and she also has good advice. She has visionary capabilities that connect many dots for you in your life. So you can have a total understanding of where you are going and where you are at. Now as for the totem pole, well this my friend is related to past life and planets that you have been to. As you can see, the quili bear, that means for many lifetimes your journeys were with other star system and have been to other galaxy. now the eagle in this case, that means you have been an ascendant master in other realm, and the wolf in this case meaning you have yourself been a protector also. In other realm, now as for the plan of reality and the Egyptian symbols well that is related to ability to communion with life and the reality that which you are into...so there for to you all is good. Be well dear heart. salamat gurin jirin... beloved..

Mary Dunahue Sunday, 11/26/00, 9:22 PM i'd love to have an

aura reading but I do have trouble reading the pages with your instructions, the dark green and blue is difficult for me. Seems like a great site. Blessed Be, Mary D

Example 29:

Andrea's Reading

Kosol: Hello beloved how are you? I know you are doing ok. In a way. Ok beloved let's begin. There is some disturbance I 'm picking up from your fields, like you are hurt on the feeling level. In this scenery I see a brown haired women crying (this is what happens when a relation has been transformed into a new one as well this mean you have lost part of your self to someone and that someone did not return a positive feed back and thus you feel the loneliness, like they abandoned you). Like the feeling of being abandoned. And it appears that the crying is helping this being who represents you right now. Ok beloved your fields are blue, and also with cloudy red. Now there is the sun and solar system approaching this horizon. Ok let me explain what all of this means. The blue in here means that you are going away and that means friends and family can't come with you on this new journey. So you are to feel the lost of many people as well as all that you have with them. So is a required responsibility that you have to do this, by going where you are going and thus is the right thing for you to do, so you can come back greater then what you are already now. Beloved in this journey that you are about to venture on, not many of your current friends can accompany you. Only a few of your love ones can come with you. Now for the cloud of red this mean you don't know what will be the familiar challenge that lie ahead for you yet. But you are ready to do what you have to do to fulfill your desire to become the person that you need to be and the person that you are meant to be. So there is fear and excitement as well with this upcoming event that you have to go through to know who you are and to know that you are the person that you have chosen to be, beloved. Now as for the emergence of the solar system that accompany your scenery, what this means is that you must keep an open mind throughout the bad and good events of the upcoming journey that you will going through. For it is the end result that will grant you the greatest wisdom of your life time. Thus with this advancement you will rise on top of your dream and all of your desires for yourself will be fulfilled. Now, I know at this time you need time to sort things out, and especially you don't need many friends at the moment because you are trying to be at peace with yourself. Beloved I see there is no unbalance in your health. But I do see that you have concern for the love one around you, because they are concerned with you. So to help you to be in balance all will be well. Truth is that you are not being abandoned, but you have been chosen to be a great person. So therefore, this is a preparation for you to be ready. And as well... it is a spiritual arrangement. Be well beloved.

Kosol: now before you was incarnate, you by your will have requested to the guardians of angels that you life at this time should be transformed, so you can remember all that you are here to do. We are with you beloved. We now take our leave.

SELAMAT GAJUN SELAMAT JA. LIGHT BEING BE ONE.

Andrea Monday, 11/27/00, 5:44 AM Sorry posted my request on the wrong board. May I please have another aura reading. Thanks Andrea From: Switzerland

Example 30:

Abigail's Reading

Kosol: OK, beloved how are you doing? To begin beloved, let me said congratulation you are going through an abundant positive experience at the moment. Your aura is very bright green orange. And there is a bright silver ball at the left side of your head, (don't want to say that you just inherited a baby, but is a similar deal of experience). As well there is red and blue pink at the right. OK, to begin the bright orange that represent emotion of positive joy as well that you have accomplished a desire goals so during this time. You are celebrating the new journey that you are in, and also saying good bye to the old journey. Now as for the left ball that is representing a break in your current relationship from your perception as a girl. That mean dear heart you are venturing into the personal goal that you set out to accomplish and you are temporally postponing your short term desire and now you are following your life term desire instead (you are now a women of fully no longer a girls), and guess what, you have friends who also support you in this. Like you parental units, both father/mother energy is strong in supporting your decision. Beloved there is also a concern for you well being. We know like you know, there is some difficulty that you have had in the physical form that can sometime hinder you in many ways. I'm not saying that you have weak lung or heart, but this hindrance is related to emotion. That means you can be over trusting of someone and thus sometimes disappointed because that person you trust sometimes when you need him/her the most. They don't show up all the time and thus you feel kind of disappointed and frustrated. Sometimes you want to tell them that, but you know like they pick up from you, that they know you are upset with them, so is not your fault or reality fault that this happen, it just that they tried, and that is what counts, so is all good. Beloved, since you have green orange, now this green is of the heart, that mean, you spent time a lot with nature and also with friend who enjoy the same peaceful scenery. So you go out to the mountains a lot that is good beloved and you very careful about your diet all the time and what you put into your form as well. You enjoy natural herbs, which mean taking herbal vitamins. You enjoy being health conscious. Now you may have a lot of understanding of many types of knowledge, but you truly do feel alone because you want love and have a family of your own. You are looking for compatibility with some of your current friends, but no luck yet. You are trying those that know what counts, and yes you want a partner, (is NICK THE ONE?). That nick he is too much power. Oh well, is just our 2-cent. OK back to your story. Now as for the baby, we see that you have a baby, this is relationship, that you have and thus have given birth to this horizon... so from here on out it will be a new and also very interesting adventure, now you are not alone. NOW AS for the red blue pink on the right side what this mean is that it related to a guy. That you find him very attractive in form and you have emotional trust in him. Before you don't have this kind of experience with this person but now you do. It feels totally that this being is the one for you and you for him so you feel the need to be with him always and as well, he now reminds you of your father energy. So you have concluded that he is your soul mate or twin flame in this lifetime. You wish to be with him. And is all-good. We now take our leave beloved, be well. SELAMAT GAJUN, SELAMAT JA, LIGHT BEING BE ONE...

Abigail Abdulnour Tuesday, 11/28/00, 5:50 PM hey Kosol :) this is Dave, my friend Abi is having problems loading this site on her comp. for one reason or another. so i am going to cut and paste her message from IMer to here :) thanks :) Abi:: I have read some of the other aura readings you have done. I am very interested in what you do and learning more about my own aura. If you could read my aura for me when you get a chance i would really appreciate it. Thank you so much. From: Boxford, Ma. USA E-mail: hikegrrl80@yahoo.com Can we post your reading on this site? yes

Example: 31

Arvind's Reading

Kosol: hello beloved how are you? According to our celestial record your aura beloved has been read before, and yes beloved we know you have asked us many questions about certain aspects of it. And now beloved we give your update. Now beloved there is not much of a change in your development for you are fulfilling your goal. Your aura has moved more to a bright orange and green (which is a higher standard of understanding and more positive in your emotions), plus there is white (greater clarity). Whenever this color white, that is now dominant in your fields, is present, your healing from emotional needs is being full filled as well your heart. Now even more than that and bigger than ever is that your knowledge of wisdom has increased many fold. So a lot has happened since the first time. Beloved we of the angel's world have given you a reflection of your aura. Now the challenge is, beloved, you have to maintain many types of responsibility to everything that you are committed to. Beloved there is a lot of souls that are around you, that you end up being their caretaker for. There is so much active time ahead for you, as well as new knowledge and more stress, BUT also along with fun and happy times to. Beloved I know your health is much better now, then what I saw before, the first time we reflected on you. There is a much need for rest on your behalf. Beloved there is a karmic debt that you need to bring to balance that is related to wife and children. It appears to be connected to this lifetime, so be warned beloved, all that you did in other lifetimes it is time for you to be pay back in full this time. That means beloved expect to do a lot of giving and charity service from time to time. That is part of your karmic pay back. Although beloved you show sign that you understand many events, but as you may know, you also have experienced many failures in your own understanding that you need to turn into a success. First of all, don't judge according with your understanding, be open-minded always. Be respectful of all representatives of different kinds (treat all equal), for they will show you the way to the success of your desired dream. In essence I feel that you need to love more by being simpler toward yourself (in other words, be easier on yourself). As you know you demand many convictions from your self and surroundings (you have high expectations). Remember that you are a human being and that means you will experience limitations (you need to give yourself a break). Also it possibility, now be well and happy, we now take our leave, selamat gajun, selamat JA. (Light beings be one and be at peace) we are victorious together.

arvind nadar Wednesday, 11/29/00, 10:48 AM Please do an aura reading for me. Can you see the aura without the person in front of you? Anything you would like from me

Example: 32

Kosol: selemat jarin beloved, we have come to your shore to give a reflection of your self. Guardians: selamat jarin dearest Clare. We have much to share with you beloved about your self and the many friends that you want us to share with you.

Kosol: Clare, there is much to share with you, at this time we are going to share with you several type of auric reflections on you. Now let us begin, the first reading is call recognition, beloved your aura color is mostly orange but is not real clear. On top is a color that has a look like of white crystal purple, and at the bottom is dark red. Your aura show that you are a water element person at this time you will experience emotional difficulty, and are looking for spiritual relievement. Beloved, this is caused by you. Your self has taken over too much charity work of being responsible for too many. Agreement with other people karmic added with your own in your life has caused burden in your current life lesson, beloved. You are a natural helper to your self and to other, but this time you cannot full fill what you have set out to do, because you are in emotional need of support yourself. As well the orange is related to your immune system that mean you are ill right now. So you will need a lot of healing from your guide, to obtain hope back into your health brighten your atmosphere. The dark red beloved is related to difficulty that you have inherited in your life, from situation that you cannot get out of (like commitment, responsibility that you cannot turn down even if you know in the long run, that you can not complete it). It is related to caring for the well being for the one close to you. But sometimes even you cannot fully full fill this predicament situation that you have taken on due to you feeling sincere toward others. (It a soap opera time yeah). As well, there is being who is sick in your area, that you call love one. These being has been bondage to you in a karmic debt. It appear that this beings who you are responsible for are in a physical illness and health difficulty, so in turn this has cause you difficulty also beloved.

Also you have quite been in a spiritual level also, because you believe in angels, that where all of this white purple come from. Beloved this is your level one. Now as I go on, notice in this present situation that you are involve pretty much with many type of friends that you have karmatically bonded with. So as for you beloved your social life is a must, for you have developed a belief structure that mirror's the need to have companionship with other on what you do in life and after life, and where you journey, too. You beloved don't like and want to go to a place or experience thing alone, you always feel the need to check with other that you are involved in. to get their best opinion, and as well you have intertwined their existence with yours. Beloved, as for your three friends, Pete and Chris and the other, well their aura is much more like you also, very orange but with more yellow and green, that is Chris! (He is more of the thinking and as well the nature lover very animal and elemental consciousness), and Pete is very blue, as well as green (he is more of the talker and as well the poet he can dream and very well a good listener and he can show you the art form of reality he look to design things and make a first announcement of event), also the other of your friends is very green orange (he is passionate and very sincere just similar to you on the social relationship that four of you share with each other). Beloved as you can see, these three beings are in a very connective karmic level relationship with you. Not just that beloved they also are the same soul who have journeyed with you throughout 6 other lifetime also, but not on this planet only, it was on Venus, and also on saturas prime of the gaunas galaxy. Your relationship with this soul is not just on this planet only beloved. Beloved I will continue your reading with correction English version etc, once I get home, but for now I send this. To be continued, I 'm still at work beloved. But as you can see, some thing are better then nothing, I now take my leave beloved.

Guardians: dearest, how do you like your reflection? As we continued more, beloved now see, that your energy is orange and as well you have been in a karmic heaviness that need uplifting, as new creativity flow unto you beloved, notice that we of the angelic force are here with you and also will give you the needed energy and support to help you and your many fellow soul group friend along your life journey. Beloved, be in peace for we are with you. Here take our gift of hope of many color light, take it and let our unconditional love, unconditional compassion, and as well as our friend ship guide you, toward the mother /father god force in yourself and around you. Dearest we always want you to be happy and full filled. Selamaja, light being be in one and be in joy, for to gather we are victorious. Beloved.

Kosol: selamja light being be one and be in joy. (That some reading right baby hehehheh)

Example: 33

Kosol: Greetings beloved Kathy and Selamat Jarin, from the guardians. We have now come to your shore and are here to give you an aura reading. Beloved you look dandy this evening. Ok let's begin, now your aura have a picture of a little girl (represents your current development and experience). This represents you but on the right side of you this form, of this little girl, is clear with individuality. On the left side is only orange energy fields, and all the other fields are mostly yellow and white with blue orbs as well as streaming comment cords to other lifetimes.

Ok, beloved we will clarify all the above now, to you on your level from our level. Whenever you have a little girls imagery that represents you which is not complete form it means first, the right side of you is well developed. You can give and receive love very easily as well as having a very strong competitive chosen action. Your personality and aspect will mirror and favor toward your daddy character more than your mom aspect character. Since you left side is covered with orange energy, that means, beloved, you lack forgiveness and compassion for your self whenever you fail and blame your self when things go wrong that you didn't expect. So it is hard for you beloved to recover from failure, because your life is always based on competition and expectation from the outside rather from the inside. Beloved you are hurting inside because there are many issues that you have not let go and have not forgiven. As well as to not give time for your self to heal something beloved you want to forget by being not acknowledge of the many self blame that you carried, even those you can fool your friends and family. From their perspective you presented to them like you are strong and have transformed all of this burden into opportunity, in front of their eye, but the reality is, you feel like you have not, and also felt that you are a alone. Beloved, your heart desire is to have friends who can hear your story when you speak with them without you acting like you ok. As well this will affect you relationship as well, you can get along with everyone, but you can't get along with your self. So in the long run you are afraid that you many love one and friends will discover that you are not that wise or that heroic to them and your self. Then you will feel that they will abandon you and your worst unwanted desire will come true if that ever happen, which you are terrified of.

Beloved, there more, orange in your case you need emotional support from friends who are not afraid to hear you speak the truth, with out acting, but is hard for you to trust, your so call friends in reality, because they change with different game set. So you don't know if they can be trusted on the human level or not. And as well most of the time they expect too much from their many interaction from themselves and you as their friends. You are afraid that they will abandon you if you let them know your true feeling and reality of choose. So much emotion work need to be acknowledged and be forgiven and cleared on your be half by you and your environment of every day circumstance. Now as for the yellow in your case, you have to use a lot of thinking and organize choose with lots of strategy thought process, since you are in a lot of competitive atmosphere so you have to try to be one or three step ahead of your desired goal with other beings wanting the same things you want. The white represent piece of minds, that is what you want so that mean during many time your desire is to be ahead of what people expect of you, and when you able to accomplished this that to you is a piece of mind.

Now as for your blue orbs, well this mean what you really want to do if you have a choose in recreations, you love to sing as well to learn other culture and read, write as well as playing instrument, you are a lover of art and beautiful structure. The streaming comment cords to other lifetime meaning you don't forget what you have been taught by your parent and traditional reality as well you can walk in both culture modern and traditional of your specie. Well to summarize everything up, there is nothing that is heavy with your chosen life, oh by the way much good energy is already on you so your many experience of good reality is already here. Enjoy your self, beloved. Kosol and guardians: Selamat JA, light beings be one and be in joys.

Kathy Chiang
Friday, 12/1/00, 9:39 PM

Hi Kosol: This is the information of my friend. Thanks for taking the time to do the reading. And I still have some questions regarding my reading which I had posted to the other board. Please let me know which board is more convenient for you. Thanks. Sherry73

Example: 34

Kosol: selamat jarin, Ricky Knott, the guardians and I will do your aura reading for you, my friend the guardian's of aura reading.

Guardians please say hello to this earthling.

Guardians of aura reading: Beloved, greeting selamat jarin from Texas Garland. Your world is quite lovely and so are you this evening in the Canadian out back...

Kosol: Beloved we now going to do your aura reading for you. There is something we are concerned about. There is a green disformational energy at your leg's area (you appear to have physical damage in that area), don't worry we will tell you what it all means. Beloved, your aura on the first layer is red mixed with brown, as well there is a green leafy cloud's above your right shoulder and head about 3 feet about you. Your high up color is blue, silver, dark pink (this is the needed filled goal), as well; there is a green disinformation at your left leg. Beloved, whenever this coloration is in your field it mean that you are not currently healthy in your both physical and mental relationship at this current learning lesson, but take heart the guardian's and I will walk you through yourself. So here we go, please step into this interdimensional travel spacecraft, watch your step beloved that nanobot are real sensitive to human touch, and follow the guardian's and me.

The pilot guardians: greeting welcome aboard our interdimensional scout ship. We will give you a tour and a guide to your self as we travel through your life's past, present, and future. By the way, you can call me, Cooper, the word cooper came from your worlds. My earth tutor was a black American man who volunteer to teach us about your worlds and culture on aboard the biolight ship in high orbit of your solo system. He nicknamed me Cooper, meaning star dog. My real vibration is "luma hon" I am one of many Kosol's guardians. Today Kosol and I am your guardian's along with your guardians for this tour toward your self.

Kosol: beloved let's begin your travel, so have a seat, and we are now entering the worm hole, computer initiate take off mode.

Computer: comply. Take off mode is now operational.

Autopilot now activated following prearranged nav into the interdimensional wormhole.

Guardians: hang on it will be an enjoyable ride and adventure.

Kosol: Beloved when there is a green energy on the left leg's, this mean beloved that you have been in a relationship with an opposite sex, or female, in your past. That this being and you have a very connected trust, but there is a bad experience from this relationship, that has caused you/her to abruptly come to an end. That in turn has left you in a shock as well in a self-Blame State or duality where you can't easily move on or forget the relationship that you have to this being that you are connected to. Is like the feeling of owing yourself to this being of karmic debt. That you cannot or don't know how to pay back. Thus in physically this will prohibit you on many decision and event in your life of progression. This even took place in the past, but every new relationship appears to follow the same abruptness' pattern, and you beloved have run out of solution. You felt that you have lost your self. And yes you did beloved have lost your self, but not lost in the present, just lost in the past. Beloved, we have now given you a second chance to find your self and heal your memory of the experience of the past, with our guidance. Beloved the relationship that you have with this opposite sex, is actually a relationship that was continued from a past life, that you owed to this person, as well this person owed to you. But once the karmic need and purpose was served according to both of you prearranged agreement before birth as you can see, beloved she has to be taken away. This was done so you can move on. In your continued karmic learning lesson, this beloved has opened door for new lesson that you desire, before birth. But we know beloved, that you didn't see the opening door, during that time, so you begin to relive what you have lived before, and trapped in a moving whirl pool of past replay emotion and memory. Guardians and me know it is hard to let go, but remember we are spirit and light-beings once meet never apart. That is a reality that you have to learn to accept. So now please learn and assimilate the gift that you have given to this person and that this person has given to you which is the time that you have with each other and then let it go. Now let her go, and let your self go, so you can find yourself again and be one with your self in a free cooperative creative way. Beloved Rick, your pasts are now healed. I am good or what? Is all good.

Guardians: you know you good beloved, so are we.

Kosol: Then is all good. Hehehehehe

Kosol: Beloved, as for your first layered auric field mixed with brown: this means healing. Your body is not that strong in the long run of things. That brown represent liver and heart energy and is what you need to strengthen in your life at this point, this mean that you cannot eat the things you desire, as well your spiritual light is not fully radiating in all of it glory's in your form right now. Because you have sadness in you, that you need to transmute into laughter and smile. Beloved, the red is physical. You need to be communed with more friends and be more with happy people. The ones that make you laugh and help uplift your spiritual, be with story teller and creativity, children, beloved this is the energy that you need in order for you to be healed and cured of your sadness and heavy feelings that you have been subject to. As well beloved, you need to visit the water devas, as well as the rock devas, they will enrich your energy back, you live close to their kingdom. Go to the river and go to the rock area, and ask the guardians angel. So ask the river and rock devas, to give you the rock and river healing energy which they uphold, channel, and will freely give to you if you desire it, just ask them to so you can be fully restored. Beloved let your life be lighted once more and forever toward happiness.

Kosol: the green leafy cloud, this beloved, is related to the father side (some how you have you father spiritual energy helping you so he is like a guardian angel to you), there appear to be an sympathetic group of being that seem to care very much about you, they are like doctor angel, nurses, and spiritual as well as compassionate friend's that is not from our earthly world's this beings whom you also see, and feel, most of the time, are actually your parent, is kind of hard to understand but they appear to see you as their son and student, so I call them your spiritual parent. They are involved in your healing as well as show up to teach you in the dream or astral worlds. They radiate light blue, pink, energy fields. They can speak and be telepathic with you, so there is female also in here, but the male guardians is more. As well they appear to protect you from certain memory, of unpleasantness, they are karmatically bonded with you, this are you many friend's from different life time, as well as you several karmic wife from other life time and son and teacher. who during this lifetime did not incarnate with you, instead they stayed behind to guide you from their spiritual plane. So it is all good.

Kosol: now as for the blue silver dark pink, wow this is tremendous, beloved, this blue, show that you are committed in your goal of spiritual endeavors and quest toward full filling your goal to be well. The silver represents hope, as well dark, pink represent peace, that you desire. Beloved your life from beginning to end has been very extreme in a way. So therefore, everything for you has to be done in a hard way. These four colors in your higher band show that you have much needed assistance from your many allies on this world as well as from the other worlds. So now you can completely integrate yourself and move on. You wish pretty much sometimes to be left alone. But that is not your nature, you are addictive to beings who you are and are committed to. So you need to take a break from being your limited self, and now is time to flow with the spiritual light of you unlimited self, just do this for me beloved, just laugh and smile. That's all. (From responsibility, to hope, to peace, and to forgiven,)

Now beloved we are now landing back to the point we started, I hope this will help you more in your quest of being.

so thank you for flying Kosol polgarians/sirian/pleadian allience star fleet.

guardians/kosol: selamat ja selamat gajun.

Liz: Nice jobs guys. Love you Rick!

Example: 35

Kosol: Selamat jarin Colleen. The guardians and I are here today to bring you aura reading of you. Are you ready beloved? Well, I know you are, as well as here, the guardians of aura reading.

Guardians of aura reading: Dearest, selamat jarin. Greetings from Kosol's home, Garland, Texas. We know how you are, and as well we are here and have heard your desire as well as your request. As before we have to come to your shore to assist you, as in the past and also in the current living present and the future. Dearest, let's begin this aura reading journey together now. Here is your reflection from us.

Kosol: Beloved your aura today is light orange (meaning emotional journey that needs to be cleared and shared with love so that you and your loved one can acknowledge the truth). Also there is a green hole from your right upper side at the head area (this represents that your love affair with a male friend has been torn out from you because you find out that he has lied to you with his actions and thus you are hurt. You know now that trust no longer has the same value in the current relationship. Remember everyday is a new day). On the outer right of your field, beloved, is purple blue (spiritual responsibility). Also there is a fairy type of energy. This fairy is about ten feet tall. She is wearing a light blue jump suit and she wears what appears to be psychotronic technology on her head. This energy is related to your field also. (It means you have seen a counselor of relationship and health wise).

Kosol: Beloved we have a situation with your fields. Your field is damaged (because of bad reaction to a relationship that has caused you to abandon some of your creative aspect). You need to retrieve yourself back and integrate with light /love again in the upper area. You are also losing different energy (you are not at peace completely), from your heart and emotional level. That means, beloved, you are feeling weak in your astral form as well your physical form and that you will be tired easily at this timeline. So don't do anything that will exalt you, you need rest. This orange color is related to a state of need. You need to be surrounded with people, who can love you and not abuse you in this emotional area, for you have been abused in this emotional level. This is why your field is so light orange. You have a desire in your soul matrix to be loved on this level. That is to have your loved ones appreciate you, and not judge you. So that why the heart area is bleeding astral energy and makes you feel tired, because your trust and hope is many times being abused by the people who you have your trust and hope in. Thus you don't feel alone. You just feel the need to be appreciated inside and out.

Kosol: beloved there is more. This state of condition which you are in, is a temporary situation. Also there is someone around you, like your son or beloved one, whom you are very worried about. For now you feel relieved in many fashion, but you are still scared for this being who is the light and love of your existence and the reason for being in this third dimensional world.

Guardians: dearest, all will be well. You know that the love of Father /Mother god force is with you and your loved one, even us angel force is with you and will take care and bring the needed balanced energy to the many situations that has and will be unfolded in your many life experiences. This is one of the greatest loves that we can / have shared with you.

Beloved as we move on, this emotional condition and affliction in your life is strong and surrounds you in many area of your daily life. You need time for your self, beloved, as well. Trust in love and trust in what is good, and all will be fine. As we move on in your reading, as you can see, the green color that is in the upper side of your field is related to a guy, whom you have plugged out from your self and heart of trust. This person's action of lies has caused you to not like him any more in many areas, so you are very conscious now. When you meet or interact with this former lover/partner friend of yours, somehow the lie that this person have put on you has made you feel unworthy in many of your chosen life experiences with this person. Thus you feel the need to be left alone for now so you can be refreshed once you are clear in the reality that you are heading in relation to this relationship. Although it is tough to forgive this former friend, and what this former friend has done to you, it is over with and thus you have chosen not to be aligned with him any more until he have evolved more in his energy. Yes, even though you still feel passion and an emotional bondage with this former friend. So it is tough for you at this time to deny him and his energy from your existence. Humanly speaking you are addicted to him, in the emotional and heart area of your experience and energy exchange but it also makes you upset and mad.

Guardians: Dearest we of the guardians force want you to be happy, take heart we have power to make many things right. Observe dearest we give you a new lover energy. This being of light will be more than meet the eye. Take our energy that we give, and see all that you want to come true. Dearest, your happiness is our shared goal. He will materialize. Do you believe in angels? I know you do dearest.

Kosol: beloved as we move on, see that you forgive yourself and this other being energy. That his action and choice has put karmic heaviness and debt in your path and life journey, and thus make your life more challenging then usual. See yourself in another place and time. Find out that all you need is love, and all he need is love. Notice that both of you have shaped each other's path and life experience. As well both of you some how are teacher and student of each other as well as enemy and friend at the same time. Both of your evolutionary journey are intertwined, so there fore, balance and common ground has to be reached within both of you. Both of you want peace and some one to love, to take care, as well as receive that kind of treatment in return from the heart and feeling creativity force of love/light within. This is the common ground, which is that both of you are human, angel, as well as light beings and caretakers of planet and each other. There is no more truth then this. Look at your self, both of you walked the same path of need. Which is that need is needed someone to share love to you and you to them.

Kosol: beloved as we move on now you know that the emotional body and the heart area needs to be healed, so that hope and trust in all that is good can be restored back to you. Tell yourself you love you, and tell the one you see doing your wrong that you love them as well. Thank them for caring for you in that manner and allowing you to share with you what you needed to radiate which more love to yourself and them (they are your reminder of love, see them as that kind of mirror of reflection).

Now the purple color beloved this color is a spiritual color of dream /healing. As you know at this time your body and spiritual body is currently being healed by the fairy kingdom and guardians, since your relation to the many element worlds is strong especially the water kingdom/ plant. So you are a nature, water, element, human beings. You are affected by people's feelings. So you need much emotional work to share with your self and other as well. You need to full fill your vision that you have dreamed about, as well you have gift of feeling. You are able to feel what is true in your relationship to the loved one that you are surrounded with. Now go to the trees, and ask the tree devas and guardians to fill your astral body with green energy so your relationship with yourself and others will be fulfilled according to your desire. There ore you can be healed.

P.S. You don't need too much medicine, beloved, in order for you to be completely balanced.
For love will restore you.

Kosol / guardians: beloved heart we now take our leave, happy trailing to you beloved. Selamat JA selamat gajun light being be one and be in joys.

Guardians: be well dearest, everything will be just fine.

Colleen Monday, 12/4/00, 10:16 AM From: Taunton, MA E

Example: 36

Kosol: hello dear one, I know you have been waiting for a long time for your reading. Well, now is your chance to get a reflection of your self. Dear one your aura has three distinct colors, yellow with silver, red, and rosy purple. As well there is green bubble mostly on the right side and one big green bubble on left the side (the size of basket ball on the left side). Now dear one let's explain what this mean. The three distinct colors show that your life has three dominate personality that influences your reality and your experience in daily activity of choose. The yellow with silver, mean that you are highly charismatic, and very inspiration toward your environment and toward the people you are with, in other words you know how to make event of every day very entertaining. You like to be attracted to people and place that have challenges to you. As well you are very competitive. As well you enjoy food, and the since of bright color, whenever yellow is connected to silver, this mean you want the highest good not for only for your self but for other. You always thinking of how other are doing inside and outside. Your worst fear is being abandon by the one you have help and love. But the best things you enjoy life and the many choose that you have made you don't regret any of your choices, because you know is for the highest good from your heart and divine beings. You always like to be strong will, in supporting your self, but you don't like to be rejected, because you are a people's person. You enjoy the company of people, because you like to energize them and they energize you. You heal people by your present. As well they are addicted to you on many a level. The red, now since the red is close to the yellow, this mean that you like to mirror your environment to support your creativity. As well you are very picky of how you see your self in an environment. It must have a certain color, certain scenery, because you get weak in a place that lack color and people atmosphere. You enjoy kids, and female or male people, but you don't like a quiet place. Because you don't like to be left alone, this memory comes from other life, that you were left alone, when you were injured in a war in some other lifetime. There fore it was a most frightened experience of that past lifetime and that has carried in to this lifetime. That why you surround your self with many a friend and colorful environment. To help that fear of yours to be lessened. Even this fear also radiated toward your parent that you have always a sense of feeling that your parent will abandon you to be alone. You didn't know where this feeling comes from. But now you know, that is from your past life. Rosary purple, well, Gloria this is the color of intimacy, you currently don't have a full intimate life, whenever this color shows up, it means that most of your intimacy life is in the astral plan, you have not truly find the compatible partner of your liking 100% yet, because again is the fear, that reality will not go as planned, by your heart of choose. Betrayal and abandonment type of thought process always invade your minds. So you like to have a charismatic relationship with no true intimacy in reality only exist in the astral counter part. You want a man who knows how to read your heart and thought process without you telling him, as well you a man who knows how to speak in poetry type of language and everything that he said has always meaning. You don't mind having that kinds of private affair even if you are married. You always wanted to be love in that form on this intimacy level, but never been able to find that in reality. So your best friend will be movie and book, this hobby helps you to feel the completeness of which you lack in the real world. There is a deep desire to have kid and to travel to a place that is foreign to you. But yet are familiar. This feeling comes from the part of you that feel sad sometime and wanted to run away, because sometime you have to explain your self, and you feel uncomfortable, in that atmosphere. You wish the relationship was telepathic, so there will be no misunderstanding of relationship, that you have with the other party. The green bubble of both left and right, this related to personal relationship that you have with your father who make a big impact with you in your life, as well the many girl friends and children whom you make a big impact in their life. This mean that they made your life complete, because of this relationship, you have become of you are today because of them. 3/18/02

Wednesday, 12/6/00, 9:48 PM

You told me once that I am an ancient. Please, when you have time, read my aura and explain more. Thanks, trusted one.

Example: 37

Kosol: dear heart your aura is very cobel blue and violet white, there is green all over your fields with both green orbs (heart relations) that is big, on both side of your shoulder with cords connecting to your form. is about one foot and one half about your shoulder on both side. Let me continue to elaborate now more then ever. The cobal blue is actually longing and desire to remember that of which you are, this energy allow you to find people with like mind, that you tend to run into by your guide's helping you a lot, because you feel really connected to the guardians angels that you have relationship with. This cobel blue are relate also to your connection to your spiritual past life that you dreamed and that it influence you during this lifetime, it is very strong connection. But there is a darkness in this color also, it relate to fear, you fear dependence, that is the reality that you don't want and have avoid, that is good, because you also hold the energy of other, that other also see you as in a way very uplifting to them, although from your mind you see your self as simple and gracious. That you are just here and a friend. Also the fear relate to that other have tendencies to be depend and attached to you. And you don't like to encourage that kind of relationship. Now as we move on your goal is to have the completion of your journey coming into a more meaning practical way, that why you are experiencing, yourself a lot. Now the violet white, this is the color that relate to open mind as well healing. as you notice you are developing and are reaching out to other puzzle that you find of interest and that can be a reflection to your completion of your journey with out a disappointing ending. As some of your previous journey have encountered. The violet and white is very strong that mean, there is definitely connection to other beings that you have a higher relationship with. So your expectation of your relationship with other is more of personal and more spiritual in nature. I see that your form is weak in a way. Because of the dark energy replacing the red, this mean that you don't have all the puzzle of your life to be grounded in this realm yet. So there is much work to be done. Also this is related to health issue that your current body, can be easily sick a lot and health issue is one of the most important things in many of your agendas. Now as for the green this is related to healing, yes there is a lot of peace and nature energy in your connection to the environment, but most importantly your interest is into healing and helping other so you can in turn assist your own condition. Is like killing two birds with one stone. Win, win situation. Now there is a male and female friends who are like angels in a way to you. These beings have relationship that is very close to you. They look very distanced from you (physical location), but are at your side a lot, is like they are at a different level of existence and vibrations but they have a great connection to you, and your interact with them a lot. Their bodies look very different from my perspective. As well, they are karmatically have bonded with you on many level of your reality. Now as for the cords, is orange and green tan, well to top it all off, this two beings have a strong emotional attachment toward you and also are your guide in healing as well, and an adviser to you on many desirable situations.

To conclude is all-good. That my aura reading for you. I hope I did ok with your reading although there is a lot more, but the more I attune to you I felt very intimate with you. So I have to break the connection. To recollect my self. So during this time is mating season for us, that why I have to break the connection. Ok to continue, as you know there is many issue that you have to experience before you can truly move on, because knowledge is paramount and as well as self mastery education's. Notice how I read you I always put humor into it, as I share this wisdom also with you, never be serious on serious matter, because the journey of the spiritual reality is about beings creative/ happy/ humorous/joy like a child. This is the key of beings a master. Is to not be serious all the time only on occasion.

anneke
Friday, 10/19/01, 1:55 PM

Kosol, I am from the pagpawnt group. We had some discussions lately, but I am glad to have met you. So I visited this website and like it very much. Thank you, my brother of love and light. I look forward to receive my aura reading. In love and light Anneke

Example: 38

Kosol: beloved Jesse, how are you? dear heart we have arrived to your sacred shore to bring you aura reading, dearest the color of your aura is blue green (healing journey), there is a green ball (represent difficulty relationship that need to be healed) that is on your left side near the heart area one feet parallel to your left side, and also there is a green ball also at your right side over the right shoulder (male person who you find inspirational energy that you looked up to), as well a green ball in the right side at your pelvis (intimate male friends always doing things together like batman and robbin). The cords seem to be loose, that mean like this person was very close to you, but has a tragedy, and has caused his life temporally (this person will join you soon for he has some to do on a personal level). Dear heart let go into detail with your reading.

computer activate holodeck sweet aura reading, for Jesse.

computer: program activated.

Kosol: dear Jesse this blue is the color that represent who you are, and your life mission, that you see everything clear, in your life, also there is loneliness, and sadness that accompany you and your spiritual journey, is like this is where you have to make a decision to go on, or not, apparently you are in a transitional situation with in your life, there is one close female friends that you have very enduring bond with, some how this relationship is based on love, but lately there is a separation that cannot be prevented, is like her physical form is far apart from you and need time for her self, that you have lost her, she is the defination of your peace of mind, at the moment there is the sense of loneliness with this energy girls friend of your as well, you have sensual male partner also, whom you share very personal time and quality time with, that you and him have a intimate sharing of time on the social and feeling level, as well you have also a hero, a male hero in your life whom you admire and adore very much but cannot reach out, to this hero so you can only keep secret what you have feeling for this person, this three energy is very important in your social and relationship order, as I write this about your auric energy I notice that your blue color is become violet's(opening up with unconditional clarity) and very charged, that your spiritual energy are amazed with what you are reading, as I go on, you are a men of convincing words, as well a composer of creative musical quality (you like to speak, sing, and music), this ability allow you to have good listening skill as well a being responsible on many level toward your goal. the loneliness that I see, is that you are tired on many level, that you have to be responsible for many of your friends karmic energy, but you feel that this is your way that you show love, by carrying karmic issue on your associate karmic less on their behalf, you hope that they would carry on them self in a long run, but instead, they have expected you always to do that for them now, which you are very with and also disappointed inside, because you did it out of love, but you didn't not wanted to make a career out of this, because you want them to know that you care that why you did it, now is hard to get out, because they have defined you a carrier of their karmic pattern and expected you in this mind set to help them always, that how they see you, and you are not truly happy with this version of reality, but you feel sympathy and realize, why stop now, and so be it. now you your self are tire, because when you need someone toward your side, to freely give you energy and attention, when you are victimized on some level, there no one who would come to your side freely, except with a prize, that is karmic debt, so you feel lonely that no one will take the time to listen to your drama and life lesson and difficulty (take turn), that no one feel what you are about, that you have feeling that they don't know how to care for you, as you know how to care for them. so you feel unfairness treatment in this many relationship. that why that you feel the loneliness, in side your feeling (no you need to be healed), is like you are talking to deaf ear most of the time that no one can read your feeling and heart expression, even if you have communication with the one who you have relationship with, you still feel, unfairness energy from them, that they don't see, that you are human and have a heart, not sub servient, so every time you talk to them is like it is not talking or interaction on a common but on a exploitation for favor and service, so this kinds of energy interaction has now make you tired, on many level. so you want to sing a song or write a poem, to release your feeling. So that you can be balanced, but me and the guardians hear you and understand your life experience and situation to know that you will be just fine, you have all the answer, and you understand yourself to further elaborate, I just want to say that there is the green this green is mixed with the blue, well, we know that you support peace in your thinking and in your habits, you feel that you are the healer and who can do much to help heal the many relationship around you, but the three person who I mention earlier in your aura, show that one of them has died (relationship disconnection or contract is over with), we see a discord of the relationship cords in your fields, so is very sad, for you and this three beings, because they all know each other and have relationship, with you this die of relationship, is like the relationship with you and them has come to a abrupt end, and it hurt all party the way it ended was on a emotional difficulty for all side, so there was a many sense of sadness and feeling hiding a lot among the party that is involve(and need to be expressed so healing can begin), so much healing that is needed, and much love and time is needed over here in this area of your life. so your heart and emotional reality will be shut down for a while in this relation to the relationship, until some kind of new contract is made, for the old relationship contract has come to a quick halt end. I Kosol and the guardians know this is will be your difficulty time, but you are spiritual and

I know you will heal, and will move on. yes it hurt, and yes there will be many tear, but you are a strong person, cry you must, hate you must, but at the end, you are love, and always be that, dear heart, we hope that your heart will heal more and more after reading our aura expression of you, so how did we do...?

Kosol: computer end program and exist holodeck.

Jess Chesnutt Tuesday, 10/16/01, 12:44 PM

From: Salt Lake City, UT

Example: 39

Ben and Dad

Ok, Ben, we have to say that your aura is a very passionate orange and red, there is much white yellow and green as well the northern star blue.

Ok, Ben as you know I now going to use light language to read your aura. As you know Ben, when your aura is passionate orange that means bro that you are on a sexual and sensual journey and wanting to attract a sexual partnership with like mind people of the opposite gender. In other words in earth term you are horny and want a girl friends or lover, in this case to express your sensual reality as well sharing your physical goal and desire with this potential partner that you desire and seek. Well Ben I can only tell you there is plenty of fish in the sea. Is all good, you can have Asian or American or Latino, is all good, but I know Ben that you wanted one or many star seed female.

Well let me help you out.

Kosol: to all star seed female out there, Ben need and desire one or many of you to be his lover or wife etc. Help him out would you? Or at least show him where to go from here. Ben is 19 year of age, in earth cycle, and is very highly spiritualize and as well are hot and horny.

Kosol: ok, as I continue, the red referred to your life, during this time you are wondering what you are suppose to bring, what gift into this worlds, so in the mean time you are experiencing different journey and attracting different collective and group, you are just going with the flow of things. As well, you are just observing all that you past by, knowledge, wisdom, advice, and friendship as well different jobs experience also spiritual department. In other words Ben you are just experiencing different activity that this worlds is offering to you, so in order to awakening your own and with the activity that you have engaged in, that it will awaken your own soul gift and then combined with your activity that you learn from this worlds. So you can put your soul gift into practical applications. You can give to the worlds what it is you have come to give it, your gift of love from your alien's civilizations.

Now for the white -yellow (related to understanding and openness of mind and compassionate feeling), this mean you are hungry a lot (protein wise) that you like food and enjoys sharing eating different level of cultural food with your friends as well reading and talking inspirational conversation bring you much joy as well when you find someone that is interesting that you can't figured out, but at the end you like to hang out with charismatic people and understand that you don't taken things seriously 100% but only 34 %. The rest of you just have fun, because you understand that life is to be enjoyed and shared. As you know, many people don't know what you want to do. But most of the time you want to spend time alone, with your interests, like your book, your hobby, as well with spiritual site (web browsing). You are not a loner, you just like to have lots of personal space during this time line. But once you get your fill of personal space, then you will share your creativity with your friends. And they don't mind many time that you want to hang out alone instead of with them, because they understand you and your need.

Now as for the green, in this case, it related to your heart. That means you enjoy beings very open to many situations. You don't limit your self, but are very open minded to new and old way of seeing things. As well I am getting a strange image here that somehow, there is something going on here. I see you taken medicine for your heart energy to help it adjust to new experience. Hmmm, this means dear heart, that there is medical condition that you are experiencing temporally. In the long run you will be fine. Then you don't have to take medication any more. All it is that you long to have a compatible women to share your energy with. This is what it is all about. I kosol understand, for me I went to get married in Cambodia the arranged marriage is easier, and superior to finding your own. Besides it is all good in my worlds and in your worlds as well.

Now as for the northern blue star that related to off world's connection and technology. This as you know Ben, you have been born into a star seed family of light, so your dad is a star seed and so is you, thus you learn a lot from your dad and are inspired by him as well both of you share many off worlds activity together. Also this mean healing you want to be a healer and also an inventor, to help bring technology from off worlds into the earth realm to help people to evolve. You love to hang out with your dad, the northern star, show that you have off worlds calling a lot on a telepathically level, and are receiving off worlds telepathic transmission in your experience and want to share them with everyone throughout your expression of technology that you will invent. Well as you can see Ben, you will do just fine. You should be very happy that you have been born into a star family.

Kosol: now for you dad aura, well Ben your dad aura, is blue and green dormant, that mean he is a healer Ben, he have ability to help heal people Ben as well he is very simple in all that he do, and very supportive to all that he encounter, his heart energy is very huge and with a lot of healing superior power, with technology and love. The blue is that your dad, is very down to earth, his voice are very honest and loyal to what he do, there is much compassionate in his face and eye, and very traditional oriented by are very open and active in vision and future idea and it practical application. Your dad is not afraid to try new ideas and to better the old ones with new inspirational idea. Your dad has much responsibility toward you, himself, and to this belief of helping people. As you can see Ben your dad, is an awesome person, you should thank mother /father god that you have a father like you have now who share everything's from all level with you. Is all from his heart and love, he love you very much Ben. Not just that, he show it throughout his action and words.

Now for the green, this is the color that he loves everyone and he is a heart person and he understands the physical and spiritual science. He is a very open minded individual and he don't judge he just supports. As you can see Ben, your dad, is all good from left to right from right to left, up and down, from down to up as well also he is multidimensional. You must always Ben believe in your dad, we will lead you right always. Now Ben, tell your dad, he is doing just fine. Bro, hmm, I hope a star seed female will pick you for her mate.

Oh well, Ben, is all good. So how did I do?

From kosol ouch and the aura reading guardians and light language division.

Ben
Saturday, 10/27/01, 4:17 PM

hey kosol, you are a really interesting guy Please keep me on your list, I asked to be off late at night hehe my brain was wonky thanks Ben

From:
Canada, West coast

Example: 40

Angelheartsong

Kosol: hello dear one, I know you are doing fine on many levels well shall we begin your aura reading? Ah you don't need to answer we already know what you going to say, so let's begin.

Hmmm, dear one, their is much to tell you, your aura is very diversified, with reds as the primary color that represent very close to your physical. As well your dormant color is brown orange (emotion and nature). There is picture of symbolism, that of a female, with blonde hair wearing a pink white robe (shows understanding and clarity). She is surrounded with blue color atmosphere (inspiration toward responsibility), and on her head is a crown of daisy flower (simple and pleasant in habit). She is also holding a pink rose (a healing gift, also nurturing children) this symbolism is very strong in your auric fields.

Ok now dear one I am going to use light language to read your aura for you. When ever your field show diverie fye (diversity?), that means you are in a search, or looking for some part of you that is missing that needs to recover in order for you to find peace of mind and of body. You are trying to find people of your type and like mind to share with each other love on your level of understanding and experience. As well the red that is close to your body, meaning healing, you are worried a lot about your health and also concern of how to maintain your physical health. The color of brown orange is the color is very critical, at this time your life is in a struggling state of well beings, you have to take herb and vitamin to help you feel better. As well you are trying to accomplish a certain desired physical goal in how you look is like you are trying to watch your diet.

The symbolism of female that is shown in your aura, is the love that you have for the guardian angels and nature spirits that you have relationships with. Is also show how much you love your father since it is in the right side that your love and acknowledgment, of the love that is from your dad, is very strong. You are daddy little girls on many level. You feel admiration for your father a lot. The blue field surrounding the female figure shows you want children and to always give them full attention to their well beings. The flower in her hand shows that you have gift in herbal understanding and love science and musical instruments and song. The blond hair and crown flower show you appreciate everyone beautifulness that is inside of them no matter what origin are they from. You don't feel there is a different in people, is that you only see that they are creature of mother /father GOD and need love just like you need love.

ALTHOUGH, you can never help people to the fullest you always do your best in praying for them and always tell them that they are not alone and that GOD is with them and that the angel is watching them. On many levels you have given them inspiration to continue on their chosen journey. As for now, be careful about your health, and don't stress your self too much on how you look, for everything's is a gift. Your heart is strong, but yet you need also to be inspired from your peer. Is time for them to acknowledge of how much you love them and they love you.

Ok, that is my aura reading of you.

How did I do...?

Love from kosol ouch and the guardians of aura reading, light language division

Example: 41

Subject: A Quest For Aura Reading for Des gerty

kosol: dear heart, i got much to tell you the color of your aura is very tan, orange, white blue, and with wave, of many green tan,dear heart let me put it this way, your body is becoming light and it is clearing your old pattern of your karmic journey and integrating new one into your biological form and energy.

the tan this is related to your old belief and karmic lesson is being consciously recognized and being accepted and let's go at the same time so to make room for new one. so dear heart many friend and family seem to be distancing from your life as well you feel a lot to wanting to be alone and not because you don't care, but because you are experiencing the need to feel your individuality and personal soveinty there is many symptom that appearing your biology, that is related to new outlook of hopeful reality that is currently appearing right now into both of you personal and public life. so you will get sick a lot during this time, is not a bad things, but just a adaptation to the new energy level that is beings integrated into your current form from your light body form. there is many life changes that you are currently experiencing in your relationship with you love, that there appear to be detachment of emotion, on many level. is like what they do, don't create attachment feeling anymore toward you. you feel that for the first time, things are truly clear in your emotion and thought, that you have become individual and love. now for the orange, this dear heart, there is much to tell you, yes as you can see, that in your life you lack, love from the one you want to love, so you need to let 's the person in your life know that this is related to sensual reality, not many people know how you feel on the inside in relationship to intimacy, but you do feel the sensual love that you need to be held and as well to be acknowledged from the one that you feel intimate too. many time you act as you are strong and don't care, but in your heart you do care how the other person feel about you and how you feel about them, but you are afraid that the other person reaction to you of what you think and feel for them, may not be positive, but in reality it is positive, there is no, "Rejection" from them. you need to tell the other person that you love them, and leave it as that, and that you have accepted them into you heart chakras on this intimate level. there is no shame in loving a person. is true this beings whom you have feeling for, do also love you. other wise they wouldn't give you any attention at all. as you can see they do give you attention. so you can now move on to the next level of the journey in relationship to this emotional sensual intimacy. it is very healthy and don't be afraid of being rejected, you are human and you need love as well. every men get hungry for love, including kosol ouch, that why I said that i am david caress part 3, all the women in the planet and star system are mine, there is nothing wrong for having feeling for another human. so you see, spiritual, sexual reality, angel, aliens and human all go together to make all of us complete we are perfect throught our imperfectness. is all good there is no shame in this game just love and more love on a unconditional level. so open up your heart of expression and go for it.

now for the white blue, this color is related to your responsibility, that you understand what you needed to do and go from here in relationship toward your personal goal and public goal, you are satisfied with many event and choose that you have made in your life and are ready to accept any changes that come with the future and you have realized that nothing will ever be the same, so now you can let's go of many feeling and past choose that you have made. You no longer hold on to regret and have moved on to your next journey but you feel that you want everyone that know you to understand that you have feeling and that you care, for all of them in you own way. Although you never will admit it directly but you will show it in your own way. and no you are not shy about what you feel, but you like to keep it to your self, for you feel that only if you choose to share then you will. there many things that you like to do, before you move on to next level. that is you like to take a vacation to a desired place that you wanted to go, shall i say Hawaii. or to other sacred place that is in your heart desire. well to simply put, everything will be fine.

the wave, dear one, there will be a lot of new people that will be coming in your life, that you need to accept because you will be their leader of some sort, they will be drawn to your energy as well you will feel a bondage with them as well. so hang tight there is much more to this in your reality, just let it be a surprise. as well the many green tan, this mean that you will do a lot of counseling for people to help them heal. you are a speaker and connector to this people well beings, you are a healer my friends and your professional is counseling. there many people around you that come to you for help and you heal them in their life and advise them in how to deal with their chosen path. my friend, i know what you are now, ahh, you are a councilor and healer...you have vast knowledge in many things and in many area. ehehheheheh you trick me, now i know your aura... i like that, hello fellow super power people, well i got to go to work now, and i did have fun in reading your aura ...

hehehehe,
so how did i do? blessing from kosol ouch and the guardians of aura reading department and light division.

Desmond Saturday, 1/12/02, 8:58 AM

Dear Kosol! I am part of the Pag group and I really enjoy your stuff ... I was wondering if you would be so kind as to do one for me? Thanks ... Much Appreciated Lite Life Love & Peace Desmond Aug 29/44 11:18 DST Montreal Quebec Canada

Example 42:

Kosol: Dear one yes your aura is reddish with blue on the right shoulder. Much work needed on the father and son relationship side. Wow, dear heart let's begin. Yes you are very busy, busy and more busy. There is not much room in your life for a new journey at the moment, but you have made a promise toward one of your loved ones, that you will make time for him. You can't put it to the side, because it is your son, or best friend. Any way, you have made a commitment to this person, and I am sure you will full fill it. Remember, is hard to back out of it now you already given your words, so no matter what you must be there, or your future in this relationship will not look too bright if you don't full fill it. On the emotional level, as well. You are very active. Also work with people throughout your action. You are not a man of a lot of words but with documentation, you expect that from everyone. Now the universal expect that from you also. Is time for you to stand and show your worth to your self, and as well you know how to help commit people to many obligation but now is time to commit yourself to your personal obligation, because you never make time for your personal life on the recreational level. So is time for your self to share love with your self. Also is time to bring other part of your self into balance especially your family life and with your spouse. They need you more then ever now, so is time to replace your busy schedule life with personal life also (to bring balance), so to bring you personal enjoyment and happiness, you always please people on the public level now is time to please your inner circle also, as to give them time in your life as well. You will experience much health difficulty in your physicality due to feel of loneliness in side your emotional life and has to take many medication for certain symptom that has arrived in your life, but all will be lifted with some uplifting happiness and laughter from spending sometime with your family especially your child they bring much joy to you. Is good to be busy but not to the point you don't feel happy anymore. You know your heart and you know your limitation, don't ignore it anymore. You can't live with out your family or their love for you. Your happiness is karmatically bondage to them so take some pressure off, and schedule some time to be with them, is best that way, life is short. Just do it. And you will be reward from the guardians and family angels around you. Is all about sharing love.

Blessing from kosol ouch and aura reading guardians department and light language division.

howie
Saturday, 1/12/02, 9:03 AM

Dear Kosol! Would you please do me an aura reading. Would love it. 02.45 - 19.12.39 Denmark Love and light Horst

Example 43:

Subject: Re: Lost in Transition (your auric reading of situation)

kosol: hello, well, let me give you some insight and you can tell me if it is the things that you need. first let look at your auric field, you aura is red (physical and health) and blue (responsibility and world of expression choose) on the inside, but surrounded by orange (emotion and sensual being), all three of this color is not good condition (not healthy). that mean, the red and blue, when a person has red and blue that is not healthy, that is he or she is in a decision conflict with her/his life, in the ability to choose and take on responsibility. that mean you need guidance as well as emotional support (through this difficult time). although you are a emotional and conversational being, but you have been through a lot of abuse on the emotional level, and the physical as well as responsibility level also, there is conflict (unresolved issue). in this three level of you life where you can't carried out your choose in a peaceful way because you don't know what to do and too much for you to handle and can't say no or yes. as you know there seem to be conflict in everything that you choose and the project that you are living. the reason for this, coming from fear, and this fear are causing insecurity inside your emotional life and spiritual life. as you can see, personification of fear, have created a conditional existence where you attractive opposite. first things what you are experiencing is the result of fear, that you won't have peace on the emotional, spiritual and physical level. as you know your husband is like a momma boy, he has a individual experience, but he can't say no to his mom, this in turn become in conflict with your personal relationship, as you and i, know his mom is like a jealous mode, this is understand able, as mom in-law and daughter in law they never get along, this the pattern of this planetary consciousness. now your husband has to learn to say no when need be when he know that saying yes can upset the balance in his relationship with himself and you, as well, he need to distinguish, the different in relationship with you and with mom, there must be a balance, and don't mix the two, on the social level and emotional level. now as for your confusion in the spiritual level, is easy to fix, let the affair of the bible be in the bible, and let the affair of you be in you, for you are the reality now and not the bible. align yourself with your heart, don't let any book from a different time and culture, tell you what to do. you have a heart and a spirits, now the most important is to say no, to what ever is causing you to have fear and insecurity, is good that you pray for guidance, but as you and i know. that why father /mother God give angels, aliens, friends, and other etc, so we won't be alone, with all that said and done welcome to our forum and group. and stargate travel will help you gain the experience of meeting your guardians angels in the physical, energy, emotional, and spiritual levels.

p.s. your mother in-law, is scare to be left along and she also scare that the one she love will abandon her. so she do everything in her power to keep her security, this is human nature. remember, she getting older, and fear in side her become stronger, so compassion and psychological education is needed, although she may be stubborn in accepting common help, because she is scare to move out of her feared condition. forgive her and pray for her. don't forget to give yourself love and her too. for all of you need space right now to heal and to know yourself more. you are not alone now. be at peace with love from kosol ouch.

Subject: Right on the money

That was amazing. I can't believe how true that was. Thank you for your advice. It's kind of weird to have read that considering I have been thinking of my dad a lot lately. Thank you again. I will definitely try and work out my issues with my father. I didn't realize that the issues with my father have had that much of an effect on me. This was definitely a reality check to read this. I hope more people post their experiences for those of us who are still kind of on the outside wondering what all is to come for us if we start to get serious about practicing the stargating method.

Jami

Example: 44

Subject: Re: hey kosol (sister aura)

well, tim, there is many things that i know from your sister, her aura is red orange (passionate in nature), but with lots of bring yellow (logic and liner) white (clarity and understanding) surrounding it. this mean, that your sister have a very logical mind and a gift of understanding new idea and making it practical. but i am concern about her emotional body those, it supposed to be orange, but instead it is wobbling (exhausted and not fully balance due to stress)and fill with red (need lots of vitamin and rest), when this happen that mean that her emotional life is not balance she don't take time out to recharge herself and she doesn't make space for herself, so she can't catch up, otherwise she will be tired, and emotionally drain, and don't have emotional support to help her ground. the redness, mean this is that is the color of health, her mind is always on the go, and she is directed by previous planning, she can't deviate from any of her sketchel. but she felt compelled to do what she must, she is passionate and never give up, once she set her mind to it. even to the point of exhaustion, your sister is very talented in logic, she can make irrational things rational and very organized in everything that you do, she live by logic, always and very organize in what she do, and also has meaning in everything that she approach and express. she is a very highly evolved soul. she is a realist type of personality and individual. she say what she see, feel, hear, smell and taste. that the way she is. she can walk with people or alone, she don't depend on no one. she know her limit and she help those who deserve her help, other than that she don't interfered. she have lots of clarity about everything once that she set her mind into doing.

love kosol ouch.

Subject: good reading again

i believed everything you said... she said some is true, and some is not... she is pretty closed minded and can't except anything that is happening to me, or is being read about her... i appreciate your support kosol... your readings are invaluable to me and my group... i am hoping to get the understanding from the guardians that you get. i can't wait to touch people's souls or hearts. you read deep into each person that i ask you to, or anyone in this forum asks you to and that is very much appreciated... you are a true patriot to our growth and our support... the info that you give is sooo helpfullll to each and everyone one of us... we have so much to learn about ourselves that its not even funny... i am truly thankful that you came into our lives... the guardians are unbelievably knowledgeable. i am so happy to start being able to communicate with them, i know you said it will take awhile, but when i was stargating today, i asked them if jake and i were going to get the house we wanted to rent, they said NO, and jake came home at 6pm... 3 hours after the fact and told me NO... so i think i'm off to a good start...

tim

VII Aura Camera

I wanted to make mention of aura cameras. Technology is to the point today where we now have the ability to capture the aura on film. Investing in one of these cameras is a great to help yourself grow and learn, and to help others grow and learn. It is also a great way to validate the spiritual side of life with actual physical proof. These cameras are expensive, but worth the investment. If you don't wish to buy one, I would advise at least to find a shop or person who has one and have your aura picture taken. It is a great experience, and allows you a deeper glance into your own personality.

If you do decide to invest in an aura camera for teaching and healing purposes, it is a great way to assist with your practice. You can actually view energy transfers during healings, and the various colors associated with them. Also, it is a great tool for students to read each other's auras, and then validate the results on the camera. These cameras come in actual cameras (still shots) or video cameras. The video cameras offer a more dynamic view of the aura and its constant state of flux. Some even come with software that will analyze your aura based on its colors. I just wanted to mention this technology as a way of assisting in your own personal growth and learning.

VIII Healing

The Healing Method is very simple. It is the same as the Stargate Method except you will be placing your hands on the recipient of the healing.

(tongue to roof of mouth)

Healer! Remember to keep your tongue touching the roof of your mouth to complete the energy circuit in your body and also to make sure you're not using your mouth to speak or breath.

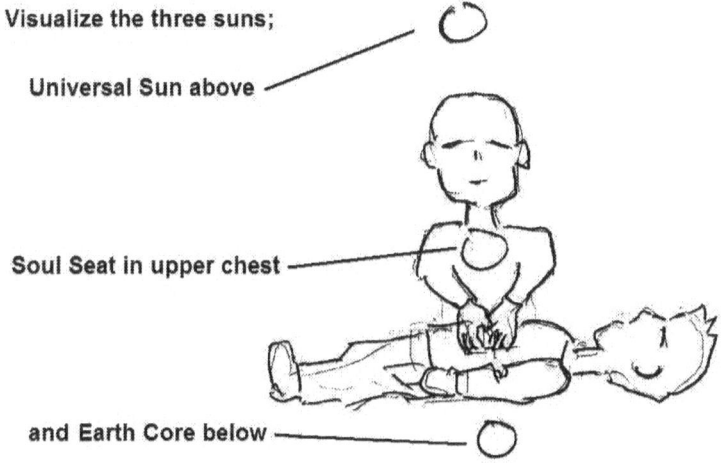

Visualize the three suns;

Universal Sun above

Soul Seat in upper chest

and Earth Core below

Envision your guardian angels all around you and the recipient of the healing. You may see the angels giving you light energy for you to heal with or sometimes even healing the subject directly.

They have been observed removing lower fourth dimensional parasites from people and performing what looks like surgery and fixing peoples insides.

The patient should just be relaxed or even take a nap.

They may also see the Stargate and experience travel although this is not the specific goal of the healing.

As with Stargate Method, inhale, draw light energy (green color is good for healing) from lower sun into soul seat, hold, chant Mantra and release, allowing the energy to flow down your arms and into the patient through your hands (you have a minor chakra in each palm.) Do a good number of cycles, about 15-30 then ask the guardian angels to help you heal your subject. Fill them with love.

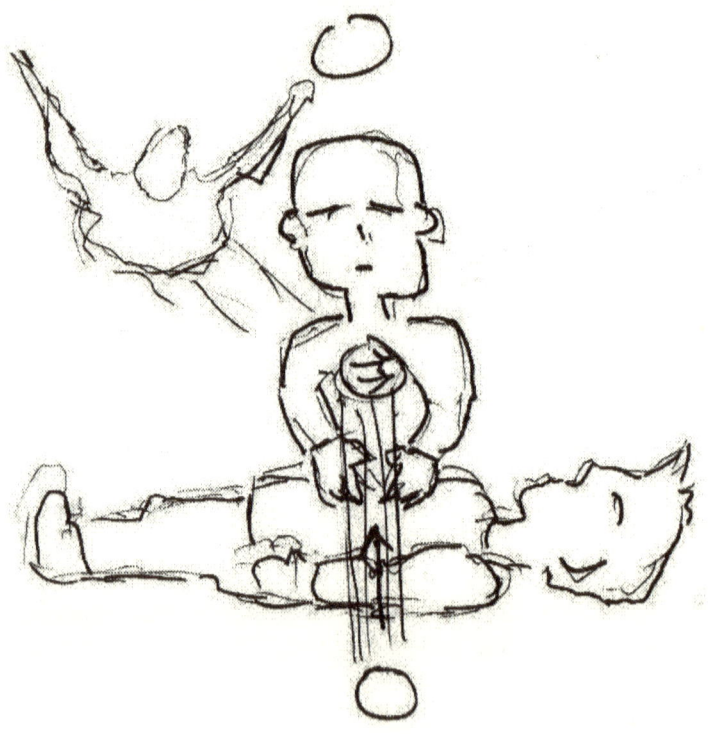

Repeat with the upper sun. Again ask the guardian angels to help you heal whatever area needs healing. If you are able to see aura you can see what areas are unbalanced or need special attention. Also try asking your guardians to show you where to apply healing.

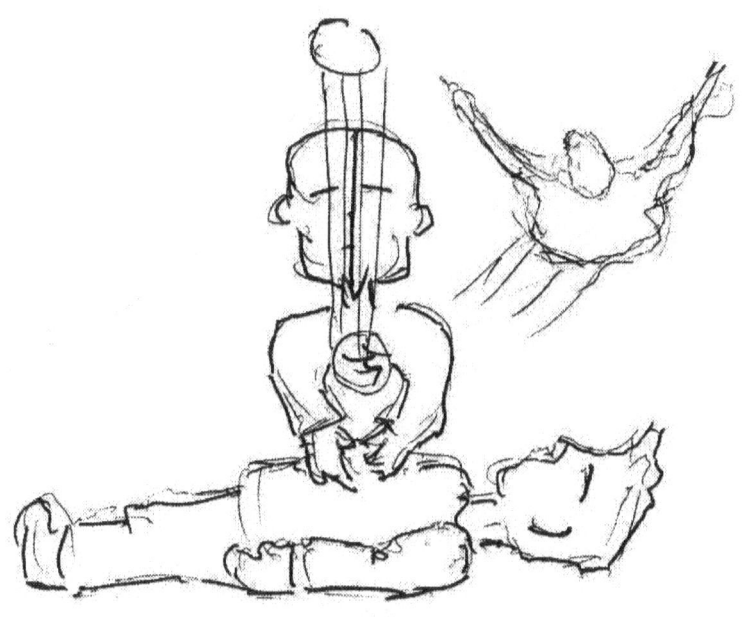

Follow up with some holding breaths and then at least triple the number of cooling breaths. Say if you're doing about 20 cycles lower, upper, holding breaths, then do at least 60 or more cooling breaths or until you begin to get tired. If you feel your aura weakening and feel tired, either end the healing session or start over from the beginning. Recharge and start the whole cycle over again.

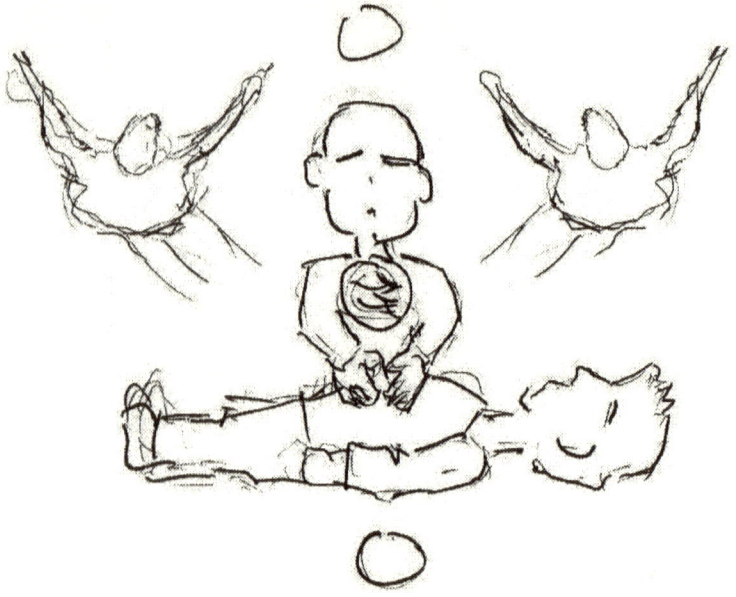

This method has already proven to be a very powerful healing tool. Always ask your angels for guidance and assistance, their technology is mostly beyond our comprehension.

All you need to worry about as a healer is channeling love energy (the energy of the universe and all existence) to your subject.

This simple healing technique is more effective than anything. It can cure all disease and even heal brain damage and genetic manipulation.

IX   Personal Testimonies

Just to give you a better idea about myself and how I try and help people, I've asked some people to write their testimony of how they met me and how it has helped them. I just want to share with you how this knowledge can help benefit others, while also giving you an idea of what I'm about. Once you learn to see and read auras, and develop and use your other gifts, I hope you make an effort to meet and teach others so that this knowledge can be shared so everyone can benefit.

Tim

Funny story I suppose, Jake and my sister and my girlfriend at the time were shooting pool and drinking and Jake started talking about this guy he worked with named Kosol. For about an hour Jake was telling us all about the conversations he had with the guy and all the stuff he was saying was almost unbelievable. He said this guy gave him an aura reading and was telling him all this next level stuff, I could hardly believe it, I remember saying, NOWAY... NOWAY... YOUR CRAZY... haha... stuff like that... I've always had an open mind, so I didn't dismiss anything he said, just kind of put it on the back burner after that night. Maybe a week later, he asked me if I wanted to go over to Kosol's house. I said yes, I'll go over and see what all of this talk is about so I rode with Jake to Kosol's. I walked in and was introduced to a guy who is more outgoing and full of life then anything I have ever met, he had this unmistakable energy that just filled the entire room. I was shy at first, I didn't know what to think. I wasn't sure if he was crazy or on drugs or what... haha... I am a fairly laid back person, and Kosol was bouncing off the walls compared to me. Jake had asked him if he could see my aura and Kosol said yes he could. Jake kind of did all the talking for me and asked Kosol what he saw, and Kosol read my aura for probably 10 minutes or so. The stuff he said seriously blew me away, I have had tarot card readings and talked to "prophets" and what not, but he straight up told me more stuff about myself then I realized I even knew. It was awesome, I was able to realize and work on more emotional stuff from listening to him in that 10 minutes then ever in my entire life! Right after he was done with my reading, he turned to the other new guy in the room and straight up laid down the law on him, and the guy said he was 100% right on with his reading too. It was amazing. Since I have known Kosol, he has given me aura readings on my family and friends when I have asked, and the results have been mind blowing to this day, I still don't understand fully how he can give an aura reading on anybody in the entire world without ever meeting them or knowing anything about them. His auric abilities are truly amazing! and I have been blessed with the guidance and support of Kosol and the angelic team. I have seen and done things that I never knew were possible till I met him. He has taken me into his household and instructed me on the ways of Stargating and aura viewing for the better part of the past year! I have honestly never met a person who has been a better influence on me then Kosol. I feel bad for slipping back into the mundane ways lately, but I plan on continuing to see how far the rabbit hole really goes in the coming months! Kosol has really raised my consciousness to a new level, he has helped me kick my depression and open up energy blocks I never knew existed. I have not felt better in my life then I did when I was practicing his stargate method for 3 hours a day at one point. He has shown me that there is a whole new world out there, one I had no idea existed till I met him! I am fortunate to have this man in my life and I don't intend to waste it any longer!

Jake

It was early in the year of 2004, when I first came into contact with Kosol. To be honest, I didn't know who was really in front of me. I sat back and watched Kosol mingle in the crowd with his different personalities. I thought he was mentally challenged. He said something that caught my attention, having something to do with healing. So we started talking on a more serious note and I was all ears. He told me the things I thought weren't possible, were. He intrigued me with his curiosity approach. This approach is still in affect today. I will always be curious when in contact with Kosol. From that day on, I have been a student, teacher, and friend of "THE ONE". Kosol opened up a door in my life, that I have always searched for. In the back of my head, I always knew somehow, somewhere there was a higher force or God, that I thought I knew of. This was the area in my life that was lost. Kosol has given me priceless information which will allow me to become something greater than I ever thought I'd be. I know we are all great, but really don't know or remember why. Kosol and the "angel team" are slowly helping me remember who I really am and where I've come from. In the beginning, the information on the earth's history, angels, guides, and guardians were very overwhelming. My belief level was just like most skeptical people, at a 1. (scale 1-10) Now, being involved for about 10 months, my belief level is at an 8. I now realize that I was the mentally challenged. I'm now developing auric vision, and strengthening my healing power thanks to Kosol. I have a lot to learn and experience. That's why I feel very fortunate to have a person like Kosol in my life. He can guide me, answer my questions, and love on me like he does with all his students, teachers, and friends. Kosol has given me a new direction and purpose in life that I am really thankful for. Without all the knowledge Kosol has given to me, I would have been living a very empty and lost life. I couldn't turn my back on the unknown. Like I said, I was intrigued! I had to know more. This is who I want to be and have Kosol and "angel team" to thank.

Jesse

I am a professional. My job as a sports writer is the type of thing many men dream about. I am lucky and I am smart. More importantly, I know how and why my professional and personal life are fulfilling. Thank you Kosol, thank you Guardians. Thank you my guides. There is no doubt that I would not be where I am today without the teachings from Kosol and my relationship with the Guardians and my personal guides. With their help, I realized who I am, what I can do now, what I can do in the future, and how everybody in the world is connected by energy - and most importantly, love. Kosol made me realize that love is what makes the universe go around and spiritual enlightenment is the way to enjoy the ride here on Earth -- physically and spiritually. There are no words I can use to describe what Kosol, the Guardians and my guides have meant to me because their assistance in my development as a spiritual being is beyond description. My happiness, my desire to make the world a better place, and my heart have all changed for the better. I was never alone but Kosol helped me realize the Guardians and my guides were with me as well. That realization, the Earth's history, and all of Kosol's teachings are priceless. The teachings belong to the universe which means they belonged to me -- I just did not know at the time and I am glad Kosol re-introduced them to me. Kosol and I have been friends for almost 10 years and I'll never forget him.

When we met, he was at my parent's home with my uncle Carlos -- another big spiritual influence in my life -- during the early 1990s talking about aura and energy, topics which were foreign to a strict catholic household. I was a recent college grad and a know-it-all who knew nothing. My parents were hardcore Catholics at that time. (They still teach Catholicism to those who need it, but have since expanded their spiritual horizons).

The truth is, my family woke up the day Kosol and Carlos visited my home and our lives have never been the same. From that day forward, we began to view the world with our hearts, unconditionally, and as time passed, we learned the scientific aspects of our connection with the universe. I learned who the real Jesse really was and I truly loved myself and the universe for the first time. Through Kosol's teachings and the Guardian and my guides, my limitations were shattered. My heart was freed as was my mind.

My eyes were opened for the first time and what I saw was a beautiful universe, a connection with others, and inner peace. Kosol introduced me to me and he introduced me to the universe. I am a better man because of Kosol and the Guardian and I am very proud to know him as my friend, my brother and my teacher. Kosol and the Guardian speak the truths of the universe and they made me realize the truths within me. The truth is priceless and Kosol shares the truth.

Jerry

It was about 1 year ago (roughly) that I met Kosol. Here's a bit of background first... In my Junior year of college life started grinding to a halt in that it seemed so empty and meaningless. I didn't accept the life of going to school, getting a job, getting married, working until I die, and that's it. I got my hands on a book called Neo-Tech which threw open the doors of possibility. After that I started reading all kinds of literature from philosophy, to religion, science, and new age. Me and my buddy Ben would reef out and talk about this stuff all the time. Yeah yeah... I know. Anyways, I always used to be a logical thinker. Well, I still am, but sometimes that can be a limiting form of growth. No matter how "logical" I tried to rationalize things, I always had a pull towards the new ages mentality, and a curiosity in reading auras, conspiracy theories, and all that. After all, it could be logically rationalized. Anyways, one day Ben told me about this Cambodian guy that started working at the casino with him. He could read auras, and talked about all the conspiracy theory and alien information that I was into at the time, so I wanted to meet him. I hadn't met anyone at that point who was into that same material, let alone someone who claimed he could see auras. So, I met Kosol and he told me a lot about things I've read about. What started validating things for me (finally... after all these years!!!), was when he taught me about things like the Stargate meditation, and I could start to personally validate results for myself. After that I've had some great conversations with Kosol where my awareness & knowledge continue to grow. There's still a feeling in me that something is just right below the surface and I'm trying to discover it. It's a never ending feeling, where I'll discover something new and then reach that point again. I guess that's the nature of growth and learning. Kosol helped get me over a point in my life where I was searching for answers, and I feel that I'm on the right path now. So, where that path goes from here is up to me. But, he was the first person I met to not only have and freely share this knowledge, but do it in a very caring, understanding, patient, and open manner. So, it was definitely a turning point in my life.

Ben

I met Kosol at a strange juncture in my life. It would be hard to discuss the impact of our meeting without first discussing a little about myself, so I shall begin with a bit o' history about me, Ben. From as far back as I can remember I have had a severe spiritual pull coming from a place I had no idea about. I can recall early in life, around the age of 4 or so, pondering about the nature of my 'soul' and its relation to the world I found myself in. I can recall a very connectedness from my youth, a clear pathway of communication between what I knew as myself and what I knew as 'god'. That spiritual pull, as it has, pulled me through various things in life. I was a punk rocker as a teenager, then a rude boy, then a skinhead. I was in the army. I was a street tough, a reggae influenced hooligan from Seattle with nothing better to do than chew pills, drink beer and smoke pot. I was a thief, a bar room brawler, and the kind of guy you'd want to have on your good side. I was a bouncer for 6 years, and had my hands in so many kinds of illegalities, I wouldn't even be able to recall them all for you. Through of my darkness and wanderings, however, I have always had that spiritual pull, always knew that I was doing what I was doing for a reason, like, there was a cause for me to forget the light, and to revel in the dark. Throughout my deviousness and misgivings, I always kept that light deep down within me. I was, amidst theft and fistfights, an avid reader of scientific material. I poured over books on metaphysics and esoterics in between encounters with wild women and bouts of lethargic drug haze. I was all things at once, you could say. I met Kosol when this life that I consider 'of the old' was coming to a wind-down. I had recently gone to jail for weapon possession (brass knuckles, if you are curious) and was in serious doubt of all the things I once held as 'me' and 'my life'. No longer was I a bouncer, but I worked surveillance in a casino, where I had plenty, plenty of time to be with myself and all of the thoughts, feelings, and emotions that I was made up of at that time. In that time spent alone in the monitor rooms, I deepened contact with 'myself' and began to see that I was not a simple hooligan, but a complex being with a very hard spiritual pull, but I had forgotten my roots, and there I sat, every night, in a marijuana haze. I began to hear about Kosol from another friend of mine, who happened to work with him. The first things I heard clashed with my analytical, left brained self. "No way, no fucking way this guy knows what he is talking about." But I kept hearing about him. I kept hearing about auras, and chakras, and guides. I dismissed them all as I heard them, but I think this initial bit was like, to prepare me for the total life change that was to come. One morning at work, I got a knock on the surveillance room door, and there he was. "Well, here I am." I remember him saying. We talked that morning for hours, and I left feeling quite mind-blown. This guy had done for me what years and years of pondering, living, and reading could not do. He provided solid, verifiable proof that the world of spirit was in fact very real, and had told me things about myself that I never told another person. "How did you do that?" I'd ask. "I can see it" He'd reply. It was a matter of fact, the things we were made up of and had considered invisible throughout the length of human history were indeed 'there' and were indeed measurable. Thoughts, emotions, connections to others, and the worlds of spirit. Simply higher frequency bands of existence, as I soon began to find out. I thought this man was gifted, or blessed, at first. He told me "No, no, no, you can see it too!" And that was it. I was sold. I began to see what he was talking about, the fine high-vibration systems of energy and consciousness that surround us. And not just us, I began to realize, they surround, or rather ARE everything. I began to see beings at a higher vibration of existence. I began to perceive the guides, and some of the lower beings of the astral realm. I began to have so much happen to me, actually, that I needed to immerse myself in it. I needed to find out what was happening to me, but more over, I needed to find a way to expand and develop my skill, that I may know what it was I was perceiving. I have since changed my entire life around. I no longer smoke, I no longer drink, no longer smoke pot, no longer drug myself up. I am enrolled in school, studying to be an energy healer (Barbara Brennan School of Healing), and am living a healthy, yogic, and organic life all the way across the US in South Florida. Farewell my sweet Seattle home! Much gratitude to Kosol for having re-awakened me to the truth, for I was lost and wandering with a blindfold on. Words cannot express my gratitude to Kosol, and to all of my spiritual teachers - this life, back throughout beginningless time. Kosol, I am sure this is not the first lifetime we have shared together, and I pray that it will not be the last. Thank you for getting there before me and for illuminating the way behind you. Cheers!

John.

This is John. Following is how I became involved with the Stargate Ascension Project but first I must give a little background information on myself...

I am 26 years old (27 next December.) I've known all my life that something is terribly, terribly wrong with this planet. It started when I was growing up and I looked at everyone around me in the small Oregon town I grew up in and saw that everyone was miserable or at least no one was truly happy or had a clue what was going on in the world. I was always highly intelligent even when very young and was always an avid learner and excelled in school (actually I always felt held-back by school.) I grew up with my very unstable, neurotic, fanatically-Christian and ignorant mother, very poor (off and on welfare) in a home with no father although I did have an older brother who helped guide me a bit. I never fit in with my peer group, most of my "friends" were "grown-ups" when I was younger i.e. up until about age 14 I mostly hung around people in their 30's-50's (both my parents were quite old too, I was born when my mother was 37, today she is 63). I was never like any of the other kids my age and one of the most common phrases other kids used to describe me was "you're weird" and I can't say I disagreed with them very much. So I spent most of my life isolated from the rest of the world, lost in books, comics, board and role-playing games, movies, television, music and daydreams; you know, fantasy. I always had a "good heart" i.e. I never wished harm upon anyone and was never very aggressive and didn't believe in fighting or hate or bigotry or racism or war. I never could understand how so many people could be so awful and wish such awful things on others and do evil things to one another, so I withdrew from the world for most of my childhood.

As I entered my teenage years, my longing for social contact with my peers became stronger and I tried more and more to fit in with others but I found my "superior intellect" made it very difficult to fit in with most other "dumbed-down" kids so eventually I started smoking to fit-in with the "loser-crowd" who seemed to be the only group that would accept me (the so-called preps and jocks looked down on me, I had too much pride to be a total nerd and skateboarding wasn't popular at that time so I didn't have that crowd to fit in with...) Eventually I began "experimenting" with marijuana and alcohol which quickly turned to regular pot and alcohol abuse. I found that by doing drugs and smoking cigarettes and "partying" that my peers were less threatened by me and I fit in a little better than I had previously in my life. When I was 15 years old, I decided I couldn't stand living with my crazy mother anymore (I was going to kill her or myself eventually) so I decided to move to Vancouver Washington to live with my father whom I barely knew at the time.

In Vancouver I found a much different and more accepting atmosphere than I grew up in small town Oregon where people were a lot more judgmental and cruel. I had to break up with my first girlfriend who I thought I loved very much to move to my dad's and so the first year and a half there I was quite depressed and heart-broken. Being the new kid at my high school also put some pressure on me and this is the period I really began smoking pot heavily. I quickly began attracting other "friends" who were misfits and pot-heads and this became my peer-group, although I did still apply myself in school and tried to learn as much as I could. I found living with my father completely different than with my mother and I learned why they were never together very quickly. Although my dad wasn't poor or physically abusive and didn't lose his temper like my mother often did, he was extremely verbally and emotionally abusive which was a new experience for me (I mean, I was used to this kind of abuse from other kids, but not from my own parent, my mother may have been crazy, but she would always profess her "love" for me.) To make a long story short, I did a lot of things to get myself in trouble over the next few years and ended up being treated much like a slave in my new home and wasn't much trusted either. My marijuana/alcohol/tobacco consumption increased steadily over the years and I also began using LSD occasionally (when I could find it.) I also took lithium for a few years as I was "diagnosed" as having "bi-polar disorder" because my father wanted to send me to a doctor who would give me a pill to "fix" me rather than be a real parent and take care of me. Needless to say, I know now that I'm not crazy and I doubt that anyone on this planet is "bi-polar" or suffering from any of the many other "mental disorders" that we label people with who resist accepting this matrix-reality anti- civilization we live in.

Most of my high-school years were spent partying every chance I could as I found it to be a great escape from reality and also a good way to fit in and gain some popularity. But even through all this mess that my life had become, I never lost my intellectual curiosity and I still read quite a bit and studied a lot outside of my school work. I spent a lot of time at the public library when I wasn't in school or partying although I was pretty much using pot on a daily basis. Although I had a lot more so-called friends at this point in my life, I was still quite awkward in a crowd and was still commonly described as a "weirdo" or "strange" but I didn't mind by this time as I was used to it. My life seemed to be "going down the tubes" as they say and up to this point I never felt much in control of myself or the direction of my future. I had been suffering from chronic depression and thoughts of suicide for most of my life and self-hatred for not "fitting in" in the world. When I was turning 19 my father's incessant criticism and my drug abuse and prescription medication all added up to be too much for me and I decided I was going to end my life once and for all. I had said many times before "I'm going to kill myself" but I never could bring myself to do it because I always had this feeling that the world needs me or I have some purpose and if I killed myself I'd never found out what it was. But this time I was sick of the world and everyone in it and I just didn't care about anything anymore. I set out on what I thought was my final journey that would end my life but somehow, amazingly, my older brother was able to find me after a few days and stopped me and talked me into coming back home. But I had truly decided to end my life (which requires insanity to do, so I can say that I did "lose it" once) and from that point on, something inside me died. The light I held deep inside dimmed and I was never quite the same afterwards. When I got back home and over that situation I basically decided to "give up" trying to do "the right thing" with my life and decided I was just going to do whatever I wanted, whether right or wrong, to make myself happy.

But I never gained back my will to live and although I came to realize I couldn't end my life with a quick-and-easy suicide, I did continue to kill myself with drugs and alcohol. I began using harder drugs, starting with semi-regular use of cocaine and leading into a year of methamphetamine addiction, using ecstasy and lsd many times and even heroine a few times. It didn't take long for these drugs to take their toll on me and my physical health began to decline rapidly along with my mental acuity and intelligence. I kept losing jobs from ineptness due to being high all the time. I began dealing in casinos when I was 21 and found it to be an atmosphere more conducive and encouraging of my lifestyle. I realized that working for someone else was never going to get me anywhere and I eventually began growing and selling marijuana for a few years. This was a period of my life that was filled with false happiness and more money than I had ever known, but I still lacked self-control or the real will to live and the more money I made, the more drugs I did. I think it's easy for anyone to see where this path was leading me...

I eventually lost even that job and was forced to stop growing and move back in with my father and take a shitty job at a car dealership working like a slave again when I was 23. I became very depressed again as I lost pretty much everything I had gained at that time and I also started having this extreme pain in my side which I thought was my bladder or kidneys or liver beginning to fail from all the drug abuse I had done. It's important to note that this pain was constant and a daily reminder of just how bad I had screwed myself up to this point. I drifted for the next couple years, moving back to Oregon for six months and eventually decided to try to clean myself up. I read a book called The Neo-Tech Discovery and it really changed the way I thought about life and the world and for the first time gave me a reason and some inspiration to stop using drugs, which I did, for a while. I found it too difficult to give up alcohol and cigarettes however and their use eventually led me back to smoking pot everyday. Eventually I was able to find another casino job in Tacoma and so I moved back to Washington. I almost immediately started using cocaine again whenever I could afford it even though I had told myself "I would never do that again" and quickly found myself headed down the same path of self-destruction I had been on previously.

At this point in my life I was a subscriber to the belief that reality is what exists outside ourselves; you can't create or alter reality with your mind. My judgment is based in logic and reason and there's nothing I would believe in without overwhelming evidence. I didn't believe in ghosts or aliens or the "ufo phenomenon" and I certainly didn't believe in any of this esp/hsp, "auras" or higher dimensional garbage. I did believe that everyone is responsible for their own life and the choices we make. I had recently (in the previous six months or so) been learning about a lot of conspiracy stuff; secret government, ufo cover-ups, the illuminati/mystery-babylon-satanic cults, cia black ops, Ruby Ridge/Waco TX/Oaklahoma City/9-11 and how these disasters were all engineered by our (American) government, HAARP and other atmospheric- control, the weaponizing of space, the Bush family and their ties with the Bin Ladens and the Skull & Bones/Order Of Death (which John Kerry is part of also btw), the New World Order and how the rich "elite" have been planning the complete take over of this planet for thousands of years and how they plan to exterminate all but 500,000 people, the United Nations taking over America, the world centralized-banking/slavery system, the unleashing of the police-state in America and the rest of the world and even how our so-called world "leaders" are shape-shifting reptilians or otherwise under some kind of non-human "reptilian" control (even though I found this difficult to believe.) And much, much more. Needless to say, the world I thought I had been living in most of my life was very clearly to me to be a lie. What I did know is that lying, deceptive, sadistic and evil people are and have been controlling this planet at least for the past few thousand years if not more and that the "matrix-world" (i.e. the reality we're led to believe we're living in) is a total deception used to keep the masses of "sheeple" confused, diseased, weakend and stupid as to make them controllable slaves.

I began to get very worried about what was really going on in this world and now that my eyes had been opened to the deception I started seeing all around me the machinations for the destruction of humanity and this planet. I began to see very clearly the lies and how the lies are perpetuated and enforced and how the deception is really all around us, everywhere, all the time. I really began feeling like Neo in the Matrix. I realized that our civilization is quickly running out of time and I began having that same feeling that I did when I was a child that I have to do something to wake people up and help save the world but I had no idea how I was going to go about doing this, especially since I had become little more than a drug-addicted slave once again. What can a slave do to change the world? How could I start waking people up when I couldn't even save myself from my own demons? I had been becoming more angry each day, angry that I had been lied to all my life by my own family, by my so called friends and by all our so called "leaders" of the world. I was losing hope...

Then one day at work, as we were closing down the casino and I was sorting some cards at a table I noticed this crazy guy jumping around and sort of dancing across the floor; acting rather strange for this environment where most people were "down and out" drug addicts not unlike myself. I remember something from the Neo-Tech book about how we shouldn't judge people by what they say or what others say about them (i.e. "this guy's a weirdo") but by what their actions are and what you know of their character. All I could tell was this guy seemed to be very happy and energetic which is something I hadn't seen in anyone in quite sometime. I also felt some sort of "good vibe" or pull towards him though I didn't pay much attention to it. Then I overheard this strange fellow talking to one of the girls about her "aura". I heard that word and instantly started thinking, "Oh great, this guy's a nut. Maybe I'll have some fun with him," and I decided to challenge him thinking I would destroy him since I already knew "so much more" than most everybody I ever talked to. I asked him, "So, you can see auras huh? Can you see mine? What's it look like?"

Now, I was thinking this guys going to say some stupid shit and I'm going to tear him down with my "superior knowledge". He took a step back and looked at me in a rather strange way for a couple seconds and then told me that my aura was "mostly yellow except for this area (motioning to his lower-right torso) is red..." The area that he was indicating on himself was precisely the area I had been experiencing this constant, agonizing pain for the past few years that I mentioned earlier. This peaked my interest a bit because I had never told anyone about my pain, I just kept it to myself. So I asked him what that meant, not alluding or giving him any information that he had just surprised me. He said something about my chakra was blocking my energy or something. I had to admit to him at this point that I had been experiencing pain in this area for some time and asked him if he knew why this was. He replied that my "heart chakra wasn't" functioning properly due to my anger which was blocking my energy flow" and this was the source of my pain.

This is how I met Kosol Ouch.

Even though all this was totally violating my personal philosophy on life, I was getting these strange "positive vibes" from him and I somehow "felt good" about what he was telling me (versus feeling like I was being deceived or manipulated like I had for most of my life.) I decided I'm going to start questioning this guy and find out what he really knows. So over the next couple weeks, every time I saw him at work and had a chance to talk to him I started asking him about things like string-theory physics, ufos/aliens, the New World Order/Illuminati conspiracy and even the so-called reptilians (which had really been pushing my belief envelope of late.) I was surprised and delighted when he answered every thing I asked him about with an understanding and knowledge even greater than what I had on the subjects through my hundreds of hours of research and study. I knew I was on to something with this guy and when I asked him if he could heal me and he answered with a resounding "yes" I that flame of hope inside me began to burn once again. Although I was still very skeptical and really didn't trust what he was saying (I don't just believe anything somebody tells me no matter how right it may sound) I thought I had nothing to lose in giving him a chance and during these couple weeks I began to realize that what Kosol knew and what he talked about was a lot like the way I've felt about things my whole life (whether I've tried to deny or repress those feelings) and was aligned with what I knew about this world not being right.

I asked him to heal me and to teach me how to see aura like him and said he would and said something about a "stargate"... Most of this mystical mumbo-jumbo was turning me off but I was desperate for some relief from my pain because over the past couple years I had increasingly been feeling like I was going to die soon. I have had heart trouble off and on my whole life but in the last couple years it had become more intense and I had started having near-heart attacks and losing consciousness while at work several times and I was scared. I knew my poor diet, lack of exercise and constant drug abuse had all but killed me up to this point and although I no longer desired to kill myself since reading Neo-Tech, I knew my addictions were doing it for me anyways. So hear I was, suffering, near death with all hope lost and giving up on the world. Enough of the doom and gloom, now on to my experiences...

My first stargate session was Ben and me being facilitated by Kosol. All I experienced was a little tingling up my arm from my hand on Kosol's knee up to about my elbow. I kept trying to see something or imagine something but nothing seemed to be happening. The session lasted about 45 mins but just before Kosol tapped us out I saw very distinctly a face "come out of the darkness" of my visual field. It was a shimmering multi-colored sort of green and purple, like oil on the ground shining in sunlight, and it looked like an old man I would describe as a yogi; bald on top, long curly/messy hair of the sides with a long, scraggly beard and he was smiling at me. I felt a definite warmth coming from him I can only describe as a unconditional love/compassion feeling. It drew my attention and I moved to eyes to get a better look at him but then he disappeared and then I was tapped on the hand by Kosol. We sat up, I noticed I felt a little strange but good and we sat and talked about our experience. Ben said he felt something like a pumping or digging sensation going on in his belly and I said I didn't experience much except seeing the face and feeling the warmth of love coming from it. After we left, Ben and I went to go get some pot and have a smoke and talk more about our experience. We smoked a joint and talked quite a bit about things and he told me how to see my aura (as I had been trying but had been unsuccessful.) He gave me some advice and, to my amazement, I was staring at my hand and I began seeing some red-orange-yellow scintillating shards of light between two of my fingers! This was the day my life changed and I decided to walk a new path.

I noticed the next day that my pain was gone. This wasn't as amazing as it may seem because occasionally I would have a day here and there where I didn't notice the pain so I didn't think too much of it. But as the week went on I realized that it was totally gone and it hasn't returned in over three months now! A few weeks later Kosol confided in my that I had actually had a lower-fourth dimensional entity that looked like a ten foot long, six-headed snake that had been feeding on my energy and laying it's eggs in me. He said the angels took it out of me and said he didn't tell me this before because he wasn't sure if I could handle it and didn't want to scare me. I responded by saying that I had definitely been feeling like I'd been being drained for some time and that it made total sense to me and then I realized why I saw the smiling face; one of the guardian angels was smiling at me after removing the hideous thing! It also explained why I had started feeling better and stronger since that first experience.

Kosol also explained how we wouldn't be able to go through the stargate until our bodies and minds were healthy. I knew my body and mind were far from healthy and I knew I needed a lot more healing before I would go through. So the next week I asked just for healing. This time I had three facilitators on me; Kosol, Ben and James. I had some pretty intense experiences this time. My breathing seemed to change without my control, several times my breathing became very heavy and my whole right side of my body kept tensing up and my lower back also kept tensing up, without my own volition, causing me to sort of raise up in the air a bit. I would realize it happening and consciously relax but then it would happen again. Then at one point I began seeing light at the top of my eyes somewhat as if a fluorescent light was right above my forehead except the light was more golden than white. I later found out that James had moved behind me and held is hands above my head and said he was just "sending me love energy". So now I had seen a face, seen some light and experienced something strange happening in my body.

Although I was being sober for these experiences, I was still smoking cigarettes and drinking and smoking pot at home. My next several experiences didn't seem to have much effect. I saw and felt a few minor sensations but I certainly wasn't having experiences like Ben or James who were already going through the gate and seeing all kinds of things. I was getting a little disappointed but I knew I still had a lot of healing to do. Kosol also let me know that I need to quit smoking because it's holding me back from going through the gate and having the experience I wanted to have. So over the next month I kept trying to quit smoking but I was having trouble doing so. I eventually started using the recharging method at home and one day, out of pure frustration of my inability to quit smoking, I pleaded with my guardians to help me quit smoking. The next day I woke up and I had no urge to reach for that first cigarette of the day as I usually do. I was amazed. Never in my life (I have quit smoking several times before) had I just lost the urge to smoke. I began to realize that maybe all this stuff Kosol was talking about is true.

For the first two months I still had a lot of doubts. Yeah, I had a few experiences and sensations, but most of the time I didn't seem to be experiencing anything out of the ordinary. Then one day Kosol told me I need to start facilitating. I told him I didn't want to yet, that I wasn't ready and didn't understand how it works and to give me more time but he said "no more free rides" and that it was easy and I could do it. So the next week I had my first facilitating experience. I don't even recall who I first facilitated, I think it was Yohn, Kosol's neighbor. I facilitated two or three people that first day and, to my surprise, I had more intense experiences from the facilitating than I had had traveling! After that day I was hooked! I knew SOMETHING was happening by this time because I had felt too many strange sensations and seen a few things here and there that I couldn't describe or explain away. That, together with my first two experiences where I KNEW I had seen or felt something, I just began losing my doubt about the whole thing.

I got the Hands Of Light and Light Emerging books by Barbara Ann Brennan and began reading the first book. As I got through the first couple chapters began to realize that there is something to all of this, there is scientific proof that we have an aura (I had actually been noticing over the past couple years that current science seemed to be heading in the direction of proving that we do in fact have souls, something I didn't believe in before.) I began to understand how the aura works and what chakras are as I continued reading. The more I read, the more things and my whole life up to this point started making sense to me. I began to realize all those "feelings" I had about people and situations all my life were in fact real and that by my denying their validity I was denying myself my own true power. Needless to say my thinking starting changing rapidly.

Everybody else still seemed to be having more intense and valid experiences than me and although I kept getting disappointed and a little jealous, I persevered and just kept stargating and facilitating every week. I couldn't deny that I was feeling better each and every week and that all the anger I had been building up inside that was killing me was beginning to dissipate and I was beginning to feel like my old self again like I did as a young child. I could feel my heart begin to open once again and my mind kept getting clearer and clearer. After a week or two since I quit smoking (I had quit drinking since before my first session) I had a one on one session with Kosol. I had been wanting to try stargating with some trance music playing in the background for a while now because it seemed that my inability to quiet down my mind and just let the experience happen was keeping me from having the experience I wanted to have. So we tried it out. At first I had the same experience as before; nothing seemed to be happening other than feeling nice and relaxed. Then, next thing I know, I was being tapped out by Kosol and I felt as if I had awakened from a dream. I couldn't recall much of what happened but I did remember seeing a computer screen with a bunch of text scrolling down it very quickly and I could remember seeing a woman. She looked like she was in her 30's, had auburn-red shoulder-length hair and pale skin and I looked very beautiful like she had make-up on or something.

I wasn't sure what happened. Had I stargated? Or did I just fall asleep and have a dream? I didn't know. But I felt that something had happened although I couldn't explain my feeling. The whole experience seemed to last for only a few minutes although it was about 35! The next week I missed out for the first time because I had smoked some pot and drank a little bit and I wasn't feeling good so I didn't go. Those two weeks sucked for me. I started feeling worse again and I was angry at myself for smoking and drinking again. I was also disappointed that I didn't do much of anything for those two weeks but waste time. I was facilitated once by Kosol and I could feel myself being pulled up but something was holding me back. I kept trying to "push myself" through but then I would just "drop back down". I knew it was because of my smoking again and I resolved to not do it again. How could I go back to doing the things that made me feel terrible and depressed and wasting my life after having these amazing experiences that were obviously healing me and making me feel better? I guess it was just a reminder to me of why I quit in the first place and I told my guardians I wouldn't do it again, that I'm never going back to that way of life again and I just asked them to help me out and give me the strength to resist that temptation.

The next time we all met at Kosol's house I did a lot of facilitating. Then I was facilitated by James. Again, I seemed to lose consciousness and go into a dream-like state after only a few minutes. When I was tapped out I woke up and couldn't remember anything happening but again had a feeling I couldn't explain and knew something had happened, I just didn't know what it was. Then the next week I did even more facilitating than before; five times in about a 10 hour period. I finally got my turn to travel at the end of the night and this time Eric facilitated me. In the beginning, I didn't feel that anything was happening and my head was starting to hurt a bit (this could've been because I was catching a cold from Kosol who was sick for a few days.) I was just thinking about my head hurting and listening to Eric breathing and next thing I know I was gone. I thought I was asleep at home on my couch with my cat laying on my chest as I often wake up and find myself. I seemed to be having a dream about watching TV and then some other stuff happened I couldn't recall and then I felt like rolling over. I jerked my hand off of Eric's knee and he went to put my hand back and as soon as he touched my hand I woke up. I was startled to realize I was still at Kosol's because I thought I was already home and had gone to bed for the night. I asked what had happened and was told I had been under for about 40 minutes and was just astonished. I tried to recall what had happened but all I could remember was the TV, feeling my cat and seeing the same auburn-red haired woman as before. So if you're new to stargating and you're not having any noticeable experience, just give it time, give your body time to heal and don't give up.

All I know now is that something is happening to me. I have been feeling the change in my heart and soul since I began this journey and I'm feeling happier and more at peace with myself and the world all the time. I'm starting to understand things in ways I don't know how I'm understanding them, but I am. Everyday I read the books I learn something new and have a new revelation about my childhood, my parents, or some experience I remember having and I understand more about myself. It seems that the pieces of my life are falling into place more and more each day. I no longer desire to smoke or drink although I know I can if I wanted to, I just don't want to anymore. I'm starting to get in touch with my higher self once again, he's been away for some time now but it's time to stop fooling around and get down to business!

Anyone out there who's reading this and wondering what this is all about, all I can tell you is it's saved my life. It's done more than that, it's reawakened me to my purpose on this planet. Finally, for the first time since I started using drugs twelve years ago, I feel that I'm back in my body living my life and doing what I need to be doing. I am filled with purpose and excitement each day as new revelations come to me and I am remembering more and more who I am and why I'm here. Most of my life I couldn't understand why the things happening to me were happening to me, why I've suffered so much and for so long. I do understand now. I'm here to heal this planet and to save people and how could I understand someone else's suffering if I had never suffered myself? Every calamity that's happened to me, I would think, "this is the last time" but I realize now that even as much shit as I've been through, it wasn't enough. I didn't give up. I kept trying to live selfishly and say screw everyone else and I know now that I can't do that because we are all one. We are all part of the same energy and we have to take care of ourselves and help each other out when we are in need.

But I can't help you until you help yourself. Just as Kosol couldn't help me until I decided to accept his help. Just like I couldn't go through to the higher dimensions until I chose to stop abusing my body and mind. But as soon as I made that choice, things started happening for me and they will for you too. It all comes down to making the choice because we all have free will. You have to choose to continue living in the matrix world and choose pain and suffering or choose to abandon this false world and wake up to your real self, your higher self and receive the love and happiness that we all deserve and require. We all have a purpose in life, your goal now should be to find and fulfill that purpose or you will never be at peace. So if you're tired of looking at this world and wondering what the hell is going on, join us and walk with us on our journey and together we will learn, grow and save this planet and all our brothers and sisters from the darkness and suffering! The time has come to wake up and ascend!

X   Telepathic Talk

When you send your telepathic message (known also as t-mails) be sure to tell your guardian (g-mail) at which timeline or date that you want that person or particular groups of people to receive your message, otherwise the message will be sent to every timeline and other realm to find the person.

Note: positive attracts positive meaning whomever your message is intended for. They will receive it somewhere in time and the person's alternative self and parallel self will receive it to in other universes and timelines, unless you tell the guardians about the date and universe that this particular person is in. In other words, it is destination or indigenous.

Just visualize or imagine the person or groups of person that you want to talk to standing right there in front of you, about three or four feet away from you or even six feet away from you, and from there get closer up and personal, one foot whether with your eyes closed or open, dependent on your visual skill, development, and concentration in the participation of the drama. See them clearly with appropriate clothes on or just make up one and if you don't remember their faces or just simply forgot, well then just visualize a light being or groups of light beings and the surroundings (environment). Can be where ever you are or just visualize a new environment that you like or prefer. Pretend that you are in the holodeck (like in star trek) and the light being can all have the name of that person whom you forgot (like a name tag or T-shirts with that person's name written on it). If you partially remember, the light being can be male or female (then just talk whatever you think or feel, express it all out).

Remember to use all five senses in the creative thought (sights, hearing, smell, feel, touch, and taste) drama and after the conversation listen to their response (the response would be, audio, imaginary, feeling, as well as actual presentation of the event, etc.). Then after your drama, tell your guardian to send the telepathic information, of interaction, to the person and their guardians as well.

Use this method also to talk to the guides. Just use the part that says visualize the being of light surrounding you and the choice of environment that you have created from a real place that exist in third dimension right now, or some where in the future or past. You can even use an event that is in the environment from the astral plane (fourth dimension) and the fifth dimensional reality. There no limits, whatsoever, as long you like and enjoy it. Talk and express, then listen, interact with them, that's all, just like you would talk to a person and a group of people and they talk back to you. Except in this case they are guardian angels or heavenly people or sometimes also known as aliens since they are not originally from our dimension. Love and light from Kosol.

XI   Stargate Travel

(tongue to roof of mouth)

Facilitator, remember to keep your tongue touching the roof of your mouth to complete the energy circuit in your body and also to make sure you're not using your mouth to speak or breath.

The Facilitator sits on a pillow on the floor indian-style (with legs crossed) or if more flexible, lotus-style (one leg on top of the other, not crossed) however more comfortable.

The Travelers will lay on their back to ether side of-'the Facilitator in a way so that they are completely relaxed and comfortable (use pillows for head, arms, legs and back as needed) and place their nearest hand on the Facilitators knee or leg and maintain contact during session.

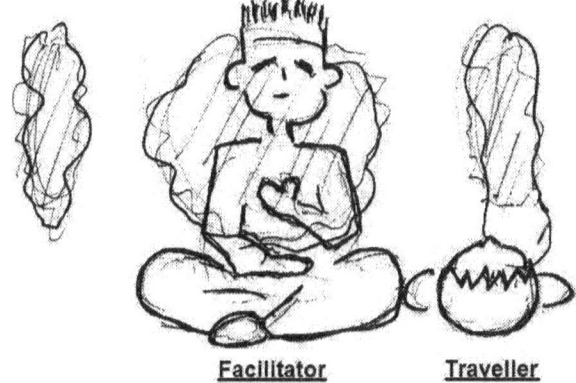

Facilitator   **Traveller**

The Facilitator (when comfortable with holding their position) will begin by asking the Travelers if they are ready. Travelers confirm with a "yes".

The Facilitator will then visualize several vortex-tike portals (Stargates) all around, above and below the travelers (one at each compass direction N, W, S, E, above and below is fine.)

You may visualize several gates or just one. Visualize them large enough for someone to go thru.

The Facilitator will then say,"Stargate open, guardian angels please take traveler through the gate." You may also request guidance/protection or any other special request for the session.

The Facilitator will then visualize the sun above his head, the Earth-core sun below and their Soul Seat sun (between the Throat chakra and the Heart chakra, at the top of their ribcage.)

Imagine all three suns spinning in the same direction (clockwise or counterclockwise, orientation is not important). Then say, "Travelers are ready, have a good experience, beginning..." or something similar to this. Hold your tongue to the roof of your mouth.

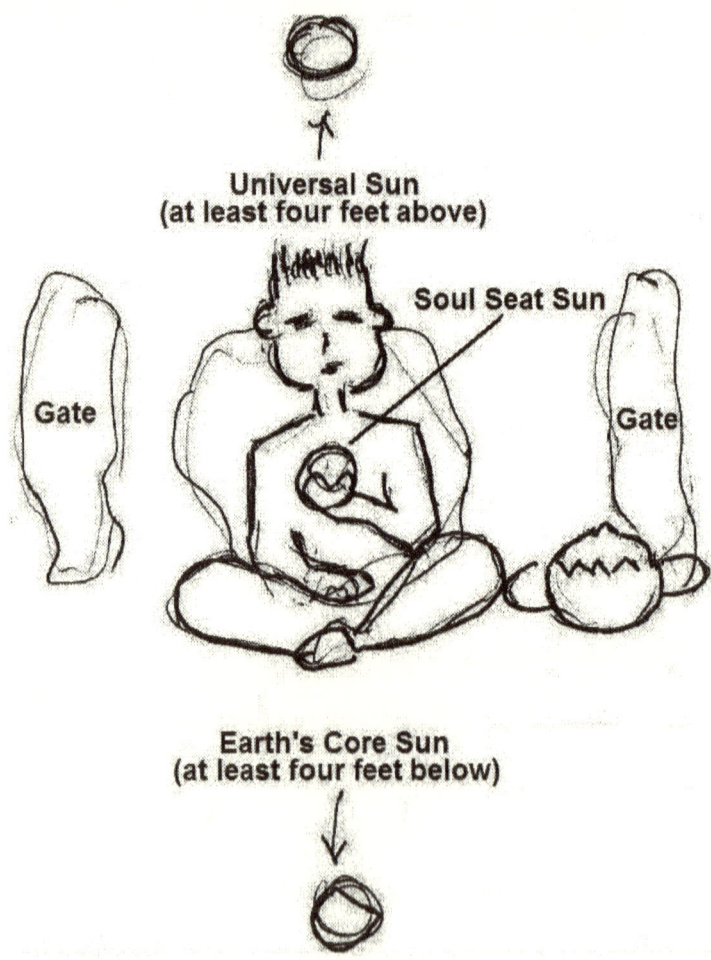

Universal Sun
(at least four feet above)

Soul Seat Sun

Gate

Gate

Earth's Core Sun
(at least four feet below)

Traveler, just try to relax and clear your mind of all thoughts. You may relax as if you're going to take a nap or focus on taking full regular breaths or focus on nothing. If you begin to see or feel something, try not to focus on the experience or analyze it by saying to yourself "What is that?" This only tends to prevent the experience. It is better to just relax and let whatever happens happen and think about it afterwards.

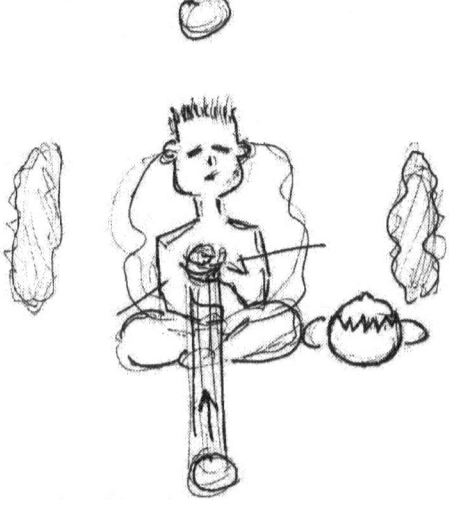

Note: Empower your visualizations by adding strong emotions of unconditional love and compassion and also a sense of peace and oneness with all life and the universe. Never add negative thoughts or feelings like sadness, depression, anger, doubt or fear.

Facilitator, begin by inhaling deeply as you visualize the golden light energy from the sun below you shooting up your spine and into your Soul Seal sun (you may imagine any color light). It helps to hold a hand over the Soul Seat area to help you visualize your sun. Hold the breath for 2-10 seconds (longer is more powerful but do not exceed your ability or experience level) while mentally chanting your soul mantra (OHM RAMA or OHM anything will work if you don't know your soul mantra). Mentally say it again as you exhale. Then repeat 7-21 times (more for less experienced travelers as they need more energy).

This is a form of guided or group meditation. The Facilitator is acting as a conductor for the Earth's and the Universal Energy Field. The Facilitator is gathering up energy into their auric field to be used by the Traveler as they need it. Only focus on sending love energy, do not attempt to telepath or anything.

Traveler, you may begin to feel the heat or 'tingling' of energy moving up your arm from the Facilitator. You may also feel your legs or other parts of your body begin to feel numb or light as if you are or are about to float off the ground. You may also see a circular gate or darkness begin to form. These are all normal and typical experiences.

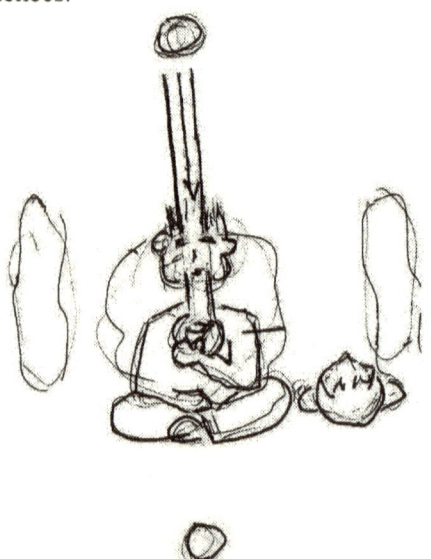

Facilitator, after you finish the tower cycle, focus on visualizing the gates and mentally asking the guardians to "take the traveler through the gate" again. Then start inhaling deeply and you visualize the golden light energy from the sun above you shooting through the center of your head down your spine and into your Soul Seat sun. Hold the breath for 2-10 seconds while mentally chanting your soul mantra (OHM RAMA) and mentally say it again as you exhale. Then repeat the same number of times as with the last step.

Sometimes the Facilitator may be pulled through the gate with the Traveler. This is okay. If it happens, Facilitator can ask the guardians to bring them back.

This kind of thing shouldn't happen most of the time but you may have new experiences with more practice.

It is even possible to gate yourself, but not at first.

Traveler, just keep yourself from overanalyzing the situation and if you do see, hear or feel something try not to focus on it. If noise or other distraction from outside the room distracts you, try to ignore it. You should start feeling very relaxed and have some sensation that something is happening by now.

Facilitator, focus on- visualizing the gates and mentally asking the guardians to "take the traveler through-the gate" again. Next you will do holding breaths which are the same as the last two except instead of visualizing light energy coming from above or below you, you will just focus on visualizing your Soul Seat sun spinning and growing bigger and brighter with each breath. Again, inhale, hold 2-10 seconds, say your mantra, exhale, repeat mantra. Repeat same number of times as before.

Facilitator again focus on visualizing the gates and mentally asking the guardians to "take the traveler through the gate". This time you will be doing cooling breaths (normal or slow, even inhale and exhale without holding.) Chant your mantra mentally once as you inhale and once on exhale or just once per breath if more comfortable. You should generally do several times as many cooling breaths as holding cycles, 20-100 or so. Just keep focusing on your Soul Seat sun spinning and maintaining it's light.

If you begin to feel drained or tired you may re-charge by starting the cycle again or bring the traveler back by touching or tapping their hands and/or the soles of their feet to ground them. NEVER leave a traveler and NEVER touch the traveler on the head or they could DIE!

Note: Facilitator ALWAYS use the Recharging Method on yourself after a Stargate session or you will get sick!

Remember that the visualization (thought) plus the emotion (love) create the feeling (belief) which allows the experience to happen.

Traveler, at this point, if you're ready to travel (physically, emotionally, spiritually) this is when most people's experience intensifies. You may see or feel yourself being pulled through the gate or have the sensation of forward movement. Remember your guardian angels are with you all the time and you can ask them for protection or to take you back at any time.

If and when you experience travel, you can pretty much ask your guardians to show or tell you anything you want to know about. If you see or hear them, ask them questions or just watch whatever they show you. When traveling, you may lose control of your body (i.e. be unable to speak or move) until you come back. You may feel like you're dreaming or it may seem very real to you. After you return, talk about your experience with your Facilitator and the rest of your group, if any.

XII Stargate Experience

Example 1:

Subject: First Time Travel

Last night i facilitated my sister. I didn't tell her anything about stargating, I told her "hey, try this out". She had no idea what was going on.

First, she saw spirals of white light. Then, streaks of rainbows. After that she saw a cave (which I think was the gate). She got a bad & scared feeling of the cave. Then, a huge black demon with a tail & pointy ears ran out of the cave, and up a hill. Then, a being of pure white energy came out of the cave and chased the demon.

After this, she was standing on a cliff over some water. Then, she was all of a sudden sitting at a table, with lots of people around. In the middle of the table was a bowl full of ashes (my mother, who was recently cremated). On the bowl, was a cloth of my mother's family crest. My sister was very happy, and very sad throughout the whole experience & was very emotional.

After I tapped her out, I explained the whole stargate process. I guessed that the cave was the gate. And, I explained that the energy being was her guardian angel. I'm not sure what the demon was... and, I'm not sure who the people at the table were.

This was very exciting & I had to share.

See ya'll around.
Jerry

Example 2:

Subject: wed. July 14th

yesterday i was over at kosol's house and i got to travel 2 times and facilitate 2 times. the first time i traveled at 5pm with the facilitation of kosol and john. it lasted for about an hour. i was getting a sensation of floating and after a few i couldn't feel their legs anymore, i kinda felt like i was one with myself and nobody else was around me. then i remember zone'n out for a few and when i gathered my thoughts again i felt this full body sensation of LOVE and compassion, it was sooo comforting that its hard to describe. probably the best natural high that i've ever experienced. it probably lasted for about 5 minutes i'd say before they brought me back. the second time i layed down was with jake, he was facilitating pam and myself. this time was crazy, it was probably the deepest i've ever been, i remember thinking damn, my body feels like its WAYYYY back there... then out of the darkness for the first time came this scene i was seeing in great detail. i remember seeing a castle up on a mountain right next to a cliff and it looked like the sun was setting because of the purple/pinkish color the sky was behind it. i remember that there was possibly a bridge coming from land on the right hand side, but it looked broken off or not complete, it didn't reach to the other side of the cliff, just then as that scene faded away my attention was brought to another scene that manifested itself and it consisted of seeing some kind of a white robot looking machine, maybe like a transformer, or one of those man driven robots from the matrix. just then somebody had dropped some keys in the kitchen come to find out and it shocked me and brought me back and i layed there for another 10 minutes before jake finished his cycle.

the only other thing i can report now that i think about it, would be for john, when i was facilitating him, i finished my first 12,12,12,70 cycle and tried to tap him out, but it was obvious that he wasn't done since he was snoring, so i continued a 5,5,5,20 cycle and with the help of pam and jake who had finished, we all tapped on his knees and feet, and he slowly came back. thats all for now...

Example 3:

the other night, jake and john and zeb and myself (tim) met up at my place and took turns facilitating and traveling. the way we did it was like an inter connected daisy chain. the first time around, john and jake facilitated zeb and myself. john and jake were in the middle, zeb and myself laying on the outside of them. i had my hand on jake's knee while john down by my feet had his hand on my ankle, zeb in turn had his hand on john's knee and jake had his hand on zeb's ankle... so it was like a big square of energy. my experience traveling was different this time then all the other times... we had Trance music playing in the background. usually i'm fairy conscious of what is going on, but this time while traveling i zoned out and don't remember much, when i they first tapped me out, i thought nothing had happened, but now that i think back, i don't really remember hearing the music for very long. i can't tell you what i experienced, because i think i was out like john goes out... that's about it for my experience, zeb and myself facilitated john and jake so i will let the others explain theirs... hope everyone is having a wonderful day!

Example: 4

Subject: today i saw the light!!

i had a big experience today while traveling. a break through of sorts. i was at Kosol's house and i received a lot of good info from him before i traveled which really opened my mind to a new understanding of this whole thing. Jake was facilitating me by himself, and almost instantly on the first breath, i took the craziest ride to date. right after the first breath, i was completely gone, my mind was at a higher consciousness, i was completely surrounded by white light. in past experiences the white light would come and go, but this time, i thought someone had pulled the blindfold off of my eyes. i saw visuals of the stargate looking like it was getting bigger or had several layers to it, but it was surrounded by the light as well. the thing that was different about this time is i don't hear myself in my head saying, well i remember this, or i remember that. this time, i was completely conscious, maybe more then i have ever been in my life, i definitely lived this experience, i don't have to think back about any of it. i saw shadows or dark beings, 2 seemed really close with a third in the middle slightly behind the others... and behind them i saw a crowd. i didn't see much detail but lots of shadows and above all their heads was the white light, like a horizon or something. then i asked my guardians to levitate my hand, and it seriously was levitated off of the pillow, that experience is hard to explain because i tried to put my hand back on the pillow, and i could do it, but it took a lot of work, it felt like the physical reality was harder to control at that point. i then asked my guardians to levitate my whole body. at this point my heart started to race and my breathing was getting deep and almost out of control like i was trying to keep up with it. i felt almost like my molecules were being pulled up out of my body or some kind of energy balls were shooting out of my body or being pulled up... hard to explain, but at this point i started to get scared and unsure of what was going on, i kept thinking, can my heart handle this, should i let it continue and see how far it really goes, but my eyes were racing and my body was shaking and i was breathing hard, so i asked my guardians to bring me back and as i asked, my breathing began to slow and i started to ground myself more and when my heart rate and breathing became normal again, i asked them to levitate my hand again, and they did :) haha... jake had his eyes open at this point and had seen all this happen and he couldn't believe it either. after he tapped me out we had almost shared the same experience, he said when he asked to have my hand levitated it did and he was also thinking about my whole body levitating at the same time i was. we were

definitely on the same page, sharing the same experience to an extent. i can see how Kosol always says this can get addicting and its better then any drug, i felt great afterwards, like realllly alive... but it took several minutes to get grounded afterwards. i had a great day and lots of good experiences. i had this feeling after talking and listening to Kosol that i really found my love for him today, i felt like i finally understood where he was coming from. i don't think i totally got him until this afternoon, i think we are both working from the same page finally, so thanks to Kosol for having me around and working with me i really appreciate it, its nice having a spiritual mentor like you bringing me to all these realizations about myself and the world around me even the one's i can't perceive yet! i think our group will be doing great things very soon! on a side note, kosol was going to demonstrate an aura reading on my aunt over the phone. it didn't happen before i left and i was really disappointed at the time, but after talking to her about it, she made me realize that i had always really loved and trusted her, and i wanted her to have an experience to validate the experiences i was having, which totally made sense, i also told her a few things that Kosol had briefly touched on about her, and she said he was so right and she will work on those things, she had also sensed him reading her or his presence when he was doing it. she is very excited to talk to you Kosol or meet you and she said her and i both need to manifest it and make it happen. i want to get her in my group. jake and i plan on stargating everyday for the month of august, so more experiences to come... love to all...
tim

Example 5:

These are my experiences from the last couple weeks, sorry they took so long.

On the 14th I traveled three times and facilitated seven times from about noon till almost three in the morning. It was a fun day! Kosol facilitated me in the afternoon for about 35 minutes. As I lay on the ground, I spent the first minute clearing my thoughts and chanting my soul mantra and asking my guardians to show me whatever I need to see. Then I just relaxed for a couple minutes as I began to feel energy moving from Kosol to myself. I just stay relaxed and focus on my breathing as I begin to feel a numbness in my arms and legs that is warm and comforting. Then I notice waves of energy pulsing up and down my whole body and then side to side and I can feel my critical mind quieting as the pulsing becomes vertical and I feel as if I'm bouncing on the floor (although I'm not moving except some light twitching.) Next thing I know I see black and some flash of a visual and then I'm being tapped out. I couldn't recall anything except the first five minutes and then being tapped after feeling the "shaking" sensations. That was the fastest I had "gone under" up to this point. I felt very good afterward and very energized.

I then facilitated three or four times and twice felt strong "pulling" sensations while about half-way through my cooling breath cycles. Then we took a break to eat a little bit. My next traveling session was Tim facilitating me (message #47) and I remember telling him that "I'll probably go under pretty fast" because I was beginning to feel a bit tired from facilitating for five hours straight and I felt like I was being pulled-thru also more than once. So I laid on the floor again and Tim began with his breathing. I remember just hearing his breath and mine for a few moments and the next I knew I was gone. I saw some images "flashing before my eyes" but they were (or seemed to be) too fast to really make out what they were. Tim tried to tap me out but I wouldn't come back which I have to stop and comment about. I've been a light sleeper all my life, had insomnia for most of it and I do not fall asleep easily and I wake up very easily (someone entering the room will wake me up.) So he did another recharging cycle and then tapped me out with Pam and Jake's help. I could distinctly feel a pulling sensation as if I was being pulled back to my body like it was an anchor. I felt very good afterward and had a strong buzz for about six or so minutes after and my body felt very light.

I can't describe too much what I'm seeing or experiencing yet but I do have faint images I can remember seeing, always see a dark circle with a light ring around it and different "energy patterns" waving which I'm assuming is my HSP third eye coming more online. The rocking sensations and the sensation of warm/fuzzy/energy flowing back and forth in my body is unbelievable. You have to experience it to understand, I can't really put it into words.

I did some more facilitating next because I felt invigorated after the buzz had worn off and did three more sessions. Then at about two in the morning Kosol facilitated me again. This time he asked the guardians to keep me awake during the experience. I began feeling the same kinds of sensations as the first two times I traveled but this time I didn't "go under" I stayed fully aware in my body. I noticed a lot more twitching and tensing up of my back which normally seems to happen when the traveler is "gone" as most people don't realize they twitch at all even though it's quite noticeable to the facilitator. I saw the gate and some strange light (energy) flowing and flashing around my eyes/third-eye. after six or eight minutes I began getting flashings of what I think were memories flashing and I could feel a tingling moving around the back of my head. The images were very fast but I was able to make out a few of them and they didn't make any sense to me, they were somehow unfamiliar, a face, a tree, a street view from above the ground, stuff like that. I felt a distinct energy move through me from the ground up and out me that was weird. The feeling I had with them was good, felt warm and healing.

Although I was awake and aware of my environment it was so intense that all I could really do is experience what was happening the only conscious things I tried to do were relaxing my body and clearing my mind of all thoughts. These experiences were all more intense than previous ones. This must be about my 14-15 traveling experience.

Will write more experience soon. Keep practicing everyone, I'm working on Stargating myself next. I just want to note that I feel the best experiences when we have 3-to-2 or 2-to-1 ratio of facilitators to travelers but the more experience I get the easier it becomes and 1-to-1 seems to work fine. I'll be exploring the next chapter of Self-facilitating and hopefully will have some good experiences this week. My job has been consuming most of my time these past few weeks and I'm looking forward to logging more time in the next few weeks. Everyone should try to have at least four experiences each week if they can. The more we Stargate the faster we heal and raise our vibrations, I know it makes me feel a lot better! Take care all! –

Example 6:

today, jake and i bought a new plant, got the waterfall working again and blessed the place. i traveled for 40 minutes, it was better then the times before today, i felt energy all over my body, towards the end i started to see some white light, i almost fell asleep a few times or started to snore a few times and came back. more to report tomorrow! Good luck everyone.
Tim

Example 7:

Hello everybody! My name is Jake Tapec. I was introduced to Kosol and the team about 2 or so months ago. Kosol, right from the gate, was very intriguing. I then started to ask questions that led me to reading the earth's history. WOW! Do I have to say any more. I was hooked on learning more about everything I was blind to. I then pursued stargating, and was very interested in learning how to start facilitating! I learned! At first, I was a little frustrated because I seemed to be getting nowhere! Little did I know, my body was just getting prepared to travel. I had some toxins I had to get rid of. Now that my body is cleaner, and my mind is clear, I seem to have a lot more focus! I'm right around the corner to going through! I feel that there was a break-through here in the last few weeks! I feel stronger mentally and physically! Stargating is now on my "to- do" list on an everyday basis! I just want to say thank-you to Kosol and the team for

giving me a purpose and the drive to do something great in this unknown and untapped area in my life!
Travel on...travelers!
Jake Tapec

Example 8:

Subject: 3 times the travel, 3 times the experiences

today i went over to Kosol's house and he had me travel 3 different times. the first time i felt energy all through my body, i saw 3 shadows of figures fairly close to my face it seemed like, felt like they were looking at me or trying to study me. i saw a few visuals, not a lot compared to past experiences. the next time almost instantly i started to see a vortex it was black and purple and multi illuminescent colors zooming repeatedly towards my face. it was like pulsing and in my head making the VROOM sound as it repeatedly came zooming towards me. right after that, i saw 3 more shadows in front of me. i think they are guardians, but i haven't been able to distinguish any detail yet or communicate with them. after that it kept going from light to dark and then out of the darkness i saw what to me looked like any old alien that you see off of the TV. it was skinny and almost stick figure like with grayish/white skin and big dark eyes. i thought i saw a few of them. i don't really know what that was all about, but that was pretty much it... the third time was the best out of the three experiences... almost instantly again after kosol started i saw what i explained to him as a panel of dark shadows, like several beings all in a row. one panel on my left and one on the right with more beings standing in a group in the middle. i had the feeling that all of them were looking at me. then i saw the vortex again zooming towards me, not as intense as the second time, but this time it was all white rings, or made of white light. it was like in the movie STARGATE with Kurt Russell when the rings dropped out of the alien ship to transport them to different places on the ship. the rings dropped around them, the vortex i was experiencing was like those type of rings zooming towards me with colors in the middle of the rings. like one after another all at once... anyways, after that i asked the guardians to levitate my right hand which was sitting on a pillow and my right hand slowly started to lift off the pillow till it was hovering in mid air for the better part of 5-10 minutes i would say. i was moving my fingers while it was hovering there and it didn't drop or feel like i would lose the feeling or anything, it was just hovering over the pillow, at this point Kosol's wife and friend came in the room and i could hear them saying LQQK at that. and then they kicked Kosol in the leg come to find out and he saw it too. that was about it as far as the traveling experiences go, i learned a great deal today just by talking with kosol. i LQQK forward to tomorrow :) all i can say is keep at it... love and light

Example 9:

i traveled 4 times over at Kosol's house today. the first kosol facilitated me, i didn't see a damn thing, Randy was playing the guitar in the other room, so i guess that had everything to do with it, but he made it up to me and facilitated me for my second time, i felt some energy and towards the middle i felt like my skin was being pulled off of my face from the middle of my head like it was being sucked through a tube or something? the third time Kosol facilitated both Randy and myself. i felt energy again and was almost going to travel then i'd come back and that happened several times. the last time "Jake" facilitated me and right at the beginning i saw some white light rings pulsing towards my head for a few, then i was seriously gone because i don't remember anything except a voice saying "HI" and it was so clear and so loud in my head i thought someone was saying that right in my ear so i came to and felt lots of energy flowing through my body, my hands felt so light i could hardly feel the pillow or jake's knee, my right hand felt like it wanted to levitate, but jake tapped me out right then. good luck to all

Example 10:

kosol: john facilitated me and jake, i was gone, in a heart beat, i was with my guardians, in a stadium or some sort, then there where lots of guardians there asking a main guardians some question and i also ask them question, then the main guardian want every group of in that room to test their ability, so they brought in a pyramid crystal that measure everyone power, by radiating their inner light strength. every group did their things, then my group guardians and i did our things, the pyramid crystal glow and radiate lots of multicolor light, the main guardians was impressed and so was i. after that i looked at the multi-sun in the sky over the dome. then i zoned out in the suns light, after that i was traveling again, then there was many guardians calling me to come to their ships, lots of them, then i ask which one, cause there is so many of them. then on of them tapped me and say this one, after that they link me up to there network of ship a i network. i was being uploaded and down loaded with all kind of knowledge and experience. it was great then john tapped me out. so i said is it morning already and lost track of where i was and what time it was. that was my experience and it was fun... with love kosol ouch the one. thanks john, your facilitation was great.

Example 11:

tonight i recharged for about 20 minutes then tried self facilitation for the first time. things were going good at the beginning, i thought i saw my guardians half way through drawing energy from my second sun, but then some punk started to ring the door bell about 20 times in a row which almost made me stop, go upstairs and knock some punk fools out;) hehe... but it was pretty much over after that, all sorts of kids were running up and down the stairs and the mom started yelling and it was just toooo noisy after that, i even had tissue paper in my ears so it would be quiet, but i could hear even through that. so i finished my cycles and i didn't see anything. i guess i'll try again tomorrow

Example 12:

was over at Kosol's for a few hours yesterday (friday) and he facilitated me first just by doing 150 cooling breath's only. i should of posted yesterday, but didn't have the chance, i remember feeling energy all over and seeing pulses of energy. after that i recharged and self facilitated. into drawing energy from my upper sun i thought i saw my guardians and then on my cooling breath's felt the feeling of being pulled forward, almost like i wanted to slump over or fall over and i got this visual of almost like traveling warp speed on star trek. i saw what i thought was stars or little different colored light traveling past me at a very high rate of speed, almost to as if i was traveling through a vortex or worm hole. after that it started to rain really loud and i lost my focus...

Example 13:

Kosol, Mike Villareal was the facilitator and Miguel and Chuy were the travelers... All three connected so well that they all lived similar experiences. Mike was able to see what Miguel was experiencing and also the things Chuy was experiencing. I will have Mike write the forum with more detail. I am guiding the group without involving myself in the travel. The guides have me recharging my energy because of the popularity we are gaining with the Therapies were are performing on the Mexican people. I am so thankful for the guides and guardians and the dolphin energy for helping me help these people heal themselves. At times I am overwhelmed by the results. But like you say I must get used to it. The guides are full of surprises and at times so funny. I am finding myself to go in and out as I work on people on my table.

Example 14:

i self facilitated today for around 30-40 minutes, the results have been the same as last time, i keep seeing shadows and they seem to be moving or doing something? i get lots of light pulses like rings in succession coming at my forehead. i see lots of visual flashes, but i can't make most of them out, i'm not sure what it is. i hope someday soon i'll be able to get them all figured out!

Example 15:

Well, I self star gated last night. I've actually been trying self star gating for awhile, before Kosol brought it up. Each time, I've had the same sensations I've had while Star Gate traveling. That is, I always feel charged & energized, like my body feels lighter & more ... well, it's hard to describe. Like at times I can actually feel myself vibrating, as a whole, but down to the smallest particle. I've also had sensations where I feel like I'm floating in complete nothingness, I lose awareness of physical sensation, but retain awareness of consciousness. Last night, when I was doing the 10, 10, 10 cycle, I saw stars everywhere, just like I was looking up in the sky (my eyes were closed). I was moving my head to scan the sky, and there some of the stars were flashing different colors & then would move & form patterns. I have no idea what it meant, but it was pretty vivid. After that, I just kind of fell asleep during the cooling breaths. But, I did have very vivid & intense dreams that night. Unfortunately, it didn't involve Jessica Alba or Kiera Knightley... they were dreams about me driving around the neighborhood. Anyways, just my experiences to date. I'm going to try & post more consistently all my experiences.

I also wanted to mention, that I've been seeing more... well, stuff. I see what looks like fire flies, little wisps of light energy. I seem them during the day, and in the dark. It's pretty random, but they just kind of float around, zip by real fast, or just blink & disappear. I have no idea what they are. Also, sometimes when I'm zoning out here at work at the computer, I see... what I can only describe as a kind of smokey haze. It's like a moving fog, but more vivid, almost like it was computer animated. It moves around in front of my face all around me until I become more conscious and then it goes away. I don't know what that is either.

Kosol, do you have any insight?

Thanks,

Jerry

Example 16:

did a 10-10-10-60 cycle on my sister today, she said she felt tingling in her head, i hope it was working, her eye sight is very poor and she gets headache's all the time, so i hope i am able to help her out... more sessions to follow. i'm going to try to facilitate and have someone heal at the same time.

Tim

Example 17:

last night i recharged and stargated, i only got through 20 minutes of self facilitation before some punk's finger found the doorbell... this was at 11pm at night. i saw black and white visuals, i kept feeling like i was falling in and out of sleep... so once all the kids started jumping around like jack rabbits, i just went to bed... more to follow

Example 18:

i recharged and self facilitated for almost an hour. i felt lots of energy, my left hand lifted off the bed a few times and twitched up and down like someone lifted it at the wrist and flopped it around. it felt effortless and light at the time, not like levitation. i saw visuals and at one point i felt like i went through the stargate, thats when i felt the energy the rest of the time after that.

i self facilitated today for over an hour, i repeated a few cycles when i could keep track of what i was doing. i felt like i was ascending or my consciousness was raised after the first few minutes, everything seemed so clear, i didn't feel like my mind was in my body, it felt higher like all around my body, i couldn't feel my arms after awhile, my body felt really lite like it was going to come off the bed. i saw lots of white visuals. i had lots of energy flowing through me, it felt rejuvenating. my hands felt like they wanted to levitate. i kept feeling little parts of my skin being peeled off of my bed in an upward motion.

tonight i facilitated jake for about 45 minutes, i think i got more out of the deal then he did. during the middle of it, i couldn't keep track of what i was doing, i saw some shadows of figures in a room it looked like, towards the end i came back because everything was so clear and easy to keep track of my cycles, i felt recharged and good after it was all said and done...

tonight i facilitated my newest member to my group Jami, we did a 30 minute session, she saw red light on the top corner of her left eye, purple circle out in front of her right eye, we did this outside, i did a 10,10,10,60 cycle. i saw some white flashes of light coming at me. and i felt really drained and wanted to slump over a few times... more to follow

i self facilitated this morning and almost the whole time through my lower sun, upper sun, and holding breaths i saw continuous pulses of white light. sometimes on the left side towards the top of my face and sometimes on the right and sometimes in the middle. it looked like it was moving back and forth. at one point when it stopped i thought i saw stars? a bunch of small white dots. i didn't see anything during my cooling breaths.

The last three times self-facilitating, had pretty much the same results as the rest. I zone in and out of consciousness throughout the ride. Today was a little different. Today I heard some whispers and felt the presence of someone or something. My hand jumped off the bed a couple of times, which leads me to believe there had been significant activity. I look forward to my next ride tonight!
See ya all "out there" soon...ekaj

Example 19:

Hello Kosol, Hello everybody This is Jesse Sanchez and I am writing from Texas. I am so happy to be a part of this forum and I'm glad each of you get to enjoy and share what's been said and what is yet to come. You have a friend in Texas and I want everybody to know that.

It's important for me that I share my/our story with the forum and tell my friends who I am and how I cam to this forum. It's also important that I share the story of how Kosol and the Guardians helped me recognize the beauty and splendor of this planet and this universe. Kosol is my best friend -- he is like a brother to me and my family and I know I would not have awakened or come to this point in my life without guidance from Kosol, the Guardians or the council.

I met Kosol about 8 years ago or maybe longer -- Time flies when you are having fun -- as a friend of my uncle Carlos, who has also been my physical and spiritual guide like Kosol. My first reaction to him for me -- an arrogant know it all college boy -- was I thought he was crazy and silly and out of his mind.

I had no idea who he was and what he was here to do. But as the years have passed I have seen first-hand what the power of our "little Genie" -- hahha -- has done and I have been a witness to what many people would call miracles and the way he has opened the hearts and minds of thousands of people along the way. Hug him Seattle, because he is very loved here in Texas and has global appeal. You are lucky to have my boy there in the great northwest and I'm so happy for you.

My boy Kosol has shown me the path to love and light. Sometimes with words, sometimes with actions, but always with love. He has never stopped my will and he has never lost his loyalty toward me no matter how far i have strayed away for women, jobs, money or whatever. I am man from God and the universe but Kosol along with my parents and Carlos are the main reason I have recognized that I am also a spiritual being. Because of him I have been inspired. Inspired to give back to the universe and inspired to reach my physical and spiritual development. I share love and light and the lessons I have been taught because they come from my heart. Kosol reminded me that it is ok and there are no limits to this universe or others or anything. He's also my crazy friend -- im sure you know -- and he likes to have fun. But he and now you guys are also a lot more.

I live in Texas and I work in the media. I am a national baseball writer for MLB.com and I write stories about men and women to inspire others. Baseball is the reason i write about the people, but there stories are just like our stories -- about love, life, universe and enlightenment.

The job I have now is something I have because I wished for it. Yes, I wished and the guardians granted it to me because they know where my heart is and what I am going to do to help the universe. I tell you this story now, because we are all family -- we always have been. I am here for you and my boy Kosol. Listen and take care of my boy. He means the world to me and he belongs to the universe. From somebody who has walked with him for years and learned, I wish you the same and the best. Jesse

Example 20:

I talked to Kosol today, he gave me some basic training that we can all start to do at home. start by recharging before and after practice. he said to put a ping pong ball in a bowl that is filled with water and to practice moving it around by using your auric field and also visualization. (for example, put the ball in the water and keep your hand about 5 inches above the ball and practice slowly moving your hand back and forth, make sure to relax and it will happen automatically, once it moves forward and back, try side to side, after that, move your hand up an inch and slowly bring your ability to new heights and continue on

until you can do it from any distance that you desire) make sure that it is a place that doesn't have a breeze flowing through or wind of any kind. once you master moving the ping pong ball in all directions desired on the water surface, then you start levitation of the ping pong ball up and down and left and right. in six weeks or so you will be able to master it. at that time, you can move to other objects as desired, it is a gift and also it is a natural inheritant divinity from a natural order. after you master the ball in the water, move it to the floor and move it around on the floor, the ping pong ball is a start, you can also use a flame, moving the flame from side to side, use a pencil, anything you want. start with a pencil, then end up moving a car :) hehe... also with telekenetic you can harness energy field and once you master it you can levitate people and also create and generate energy ball. and you can project it and cause energy disruption in your environment, this is the evolution of telekenetic, at the end would be materialization and dematerialization. that means that once you are at a certain level, say you can take a coffee table and break it down to a molecular level and teleport it to a place that you wish and restructure it through your visualization. so telekenetic evolves rapidly in 6 weeks time or so, then you will be able to understand how the great pyramids were built so easily. p.s. don't forget to have witnesses while your practice so you can have verification and validation to your experiences so people will believe you and it will make a stronger argument towards what we are doing and also so you can believe it too. practice practice practice. good luck
galacticP.I.M.P. jr.

Example 21:

today i traveled for about 40 minutes with malia's boyfriend paul and kosol as the facilitator, i saw lots of white pulses of light at the beginning, then i felt a lot of energy flowing through my body. during the middle i felt all my energy being sucked to the middle of my body and up and out of it, it felt like a huge weight was lifted off of me, i could breathe sooo easy after it. then things switched from dark to white light, and i could see pulses of light that looked black or dark blue. then it went dark again and i started to see a shadow of someone and all of a sudden that shadow turned into detail and i thought i was looking at a workshop of some kind with an alien looking creature sitting at a drawing table i thought. the machines looked like they were possibly made out of wood or something like that. real primitive looking. that didn't last for very long and i came back and just felt energy again all over my body...

i traveled again with kosol facilitating for about 40 minutes again. at first i saw light flashes again and then i saw a vortex or a tornado or something kind of swaying left and right, i then saw a big white ring that just stayed at the top of my face, i could see around all the edges of it, and it didn't move. i then started to feel my right hand levitate off the pillow, i tried to fight it and push it back down, but it was more work to push it down, then let it go up, it felt like my hand was total energy, i tried to move my fingers, but they felt completely numb. i didn't let the levitation happen this time, i tried to fight it to make sure i wasn't doing it. it hurt my muscles to try to push again the levitation. as that was going on i got a ton of visuals, i don't know what i was seeing, lots of shadows and lots of motion. i couldn't feel kosol's knee, my whole body was full of energy that felt like it was moving around. as i type now my right hand feels numb all the way to the elbow for some reason. i was asking my guardians for download information and that's what kosol said i got, all sorts of information was coming into me that i couldn't make out or understand. more to follow tomorrow...

i came over to Kosol's house and recharged and then self facilitated for a while, i got through my first 10, and 3 of my second 10 before i went through. i started seeing white visuals, i asked to see my guardians and i started to be able to make out shadow figures, looked to be about 6 of them or so standing around. i got the feeling that they were all looking at me. i could hear myself snoring, but it seemed to be way behind me, like i was really far away from my body. i actually went for a while, i saw several faces come out of the darkness. i felt energy coming into my head with lots of visuals that i couldn't make out, at one point the top left side of my neck started to hurt towards the bottom of my head. i heard kosol get home so i asked my guardians to bring me back and they did and i opened my eyes. i found out today that my step dad has two tumors in his leg, so i'm going to get with kosol about how to start healing sessions on him, more about that in the future...

i stargated by myself just now, i recharged before and after... i seriously went after the first breathe. i started seeing lots of light flashes out of the darkness... i bought a blindfold and i was using ear plugs and also i was laying on my bed. i didn't travel for very long, i basically got what i wanted... right away i asked the guardians to talk to me and they did, i started to hear different things, some i could understand and some made no sense at all... the voices sounded different... i would ask a question and it would get answered, it was kind of crazy. it wasn't a loud voice like i had heard before... it was more like the voices came in form of thought... i asked a question and out of nowhere i would hear an answer... not so much with my ears. just in my head, i know i wasn't doing it or trying to answer my own questions... the voices were also different, so there must have been several beings answering my questions. i am looking forward to traveling again to see if i hear them next time! i am also very pleased to read the questions and answers from and for my friends, jerry seems very enlightened and so is kosol. between you two it seems that most any question can be answered. so i look forward to learning more about my friends and i'll make sure to throw out questions of my own... i have traveled 3 times today and now i'm going to practice on my telekenesis for a while... good luck to all
with love,

think there is definitely value to beginning with 2 people, so that you can verify results, and have someone to share the experiences with. I just wanted to mention something to anyone who's starting out, or even done it a few times.

Words are empty, they're just a medium to communicate. Don' t get caught up in any of the meanings or stigma applied with any words regarding Stargating. The ultimate intent is to grow spiritually. The experience is what matters.

I guess what I'm trying to say, is that everything is an experience. People have many different names, terms, etc... for all kinds of experiences, and this creates structure, expectation, and then conditioned thinking. I'm not saying Stargating does that, but, just remember to have an awareness of your own thoughts, experiences, validations, and conclusions. Learning means continual growth through experience, integrating those experiences, and updating yourself based on those experiences. The alternative, is to fall into any conditioned way of thinking.

So, as far as Stargating goes, there are definitely some basic rules that should be followed for the benefit of first time "travelers". Just remember to eliminate expectation and just live the experience. The only important things to remember are the mechanics of how it's done. Even that changes for each person as you grow, but, always begin with the mechanics. Starting out with 2 people is probably best, but eventually you can "self facilitate".

When you think about it, you have all the power within you to accomplish anything. Sometimes it takes guidance, or a structured form of learning, but ultimately you have the power of existence within the very fabric of your being. It just depends on how you choose to remember that fact. So, just remember that there are many other names for "Stargating", and many other methods that yield the same results. It's a human word, being used to describe a spiritual experience, and that's always hard especially when there's such a difference between actually having an experience then & trying to put that experience into words to share with someone. Sometimes, there just aren't words enough to describe any experience, especially from the

viewpoint of each unique individual.
Happy travels,
Jerry

this morning i recharged before and after, and self facilitated for about 30 minutes. not much happened this time, i made it to about 19 on my cooling breaths and at that point i was seeing white light, it actually started about a few breaths into my upper sun cycle. but i just kept counting on through. once i realized that was about all that was going to happen i stopped counting and went with it. i felt lots of energy this time going through my body, lots of tingles and twitches. i didn't see anything, just felt everything this time. it always surprises me how each time is different, sometimes its really strong other times not a lot happens... its very humbling when you are ready for a lot to happen and it doesn't, but then the next time it does again, i guess you just never know what your going to get or what you can handle at the time. i always wonder if its from a lack of energy in my auric field that doesn't send me through as deep sometimes or what the deal is... anyways, after i recharged at the end, i felt like a million bucks... LOTS of energy was at my disposal. so i will travel again at around 2:30pm...

i self facilitated for about an hour, i recharged before and after, i made it through my lower sun, and about 9 of my upper sun before i started to see white light and some typical alien looking beings. for along time, i was really deep down in it, i was talking back and forth and hearing lots of voices. i don't remember what all was said because when i came back to, i realized how deep i was. anyways, that's all for now

aura reading example :

--well, i can tell you this, that your aura is very pink and violet dormently, but i know that your emotional body is very trapped in the frustion realm of loneliness. because there seem to be a redish glow in the second chakras area. let me tell you what it all mean. when a person has pink in your case that mean you are a

175

person who have a strong connection to the celestial realm and receive wisdom and guidance always from great and powerful individual. but not a lot on a personal level. but echo from the vision worlds. you will always long to be with like mind always feel compassion toward bad and good people. you will always feel, distanced or not belong to this time and also to the people of your kind sometime. like you know that you don't belong to this realm but you like a visitor. but regardless you are always open to everyone. now as for the violet, it means that your six chakras is open. when this happen you will always want and crave celestial interaction or people who have contact with them. you will always have desire to seek advance soul or similar reality and to connect to them, for you know that you are not alone. now as for the orange red, this is relate to anger in the emotional body. there is a struggle between the mundane way and your way, it conflict, sometime when it is in the right side it relate to you father figure as well there is unresolved lesson, that needed to be confront or forgive. even in your relationship to your husband there is always the need to confront some issue, but sometime anger begin to block creativity, when this happen, you must take a step back and bless the situation with prayer and forgiveness. so love can flow through your emotional body. and compassion and peace can bless you and your present human relationship. that you will always be in connection with the love of the father and also your mother side, with out anger. so you don't have to feel along in your difficulty it ok to love yourself for it, and forgive yourself as well the situation that has brought you there. love kosol ouch.

Kosol Wedding Pictures